Science

Level C

Alfred E. Chant, Author

Curriculum Supervisor
Fairfield School, Massapequa, New York

Patricia Grasso, Ph.D., Consultant

Assistant Professor of Biology
The College of St. Rose, Albany, New York

MODERN CURRICULUM PRESS
Cleveland • Toronto

Acknowledgments

Project Editor	Phyllis Sibbing
Text and Photo Editor	Sharon M. Marosi
Copy Editor	Anne M. DiTeodoro
Editorial Consultants	Learning Design Associates, Ltd.
Photo Research	Vicki L. Lewis
Text Design	Kenneth L. Shipley
Design and Production	Dimensions and Directions, Ltd.
Text Art	Vantage Art
Cover Design	John K. Crum

ISBN 0-8136-2509-2 (Pupil's Edition)   0-8136-2534-3 (Teacher's Edition)

12 13 14 15   99 98

Level C
Table of Contents

Recognizing Important Words

Read the paragraph below. Find the word that looks different from the others.

The moon travels in an **orbit** around the earth. The **orbit** is the path the moon travels.

Which word in the paragraph looks different?

_____

Which word is the important word? _____

How can you tell that **orbit** is an important word? It is printed in dark print. This dark print is called **boldface** type. Boldface type is one way to call attention to a word.

Read the next paragraph. Which word would you put in boldface?

The lion is a carnivorous, or meat-eating, animal. It feeds on zebras and other animals.

Did you say that **carnivorous** should be in boldface? You are right. In this book there are many words in boldface type. Look for them as you read.

Underlined Words

There are other ways to tell that a word is important. Look at this paragraph.

> The food then passes into the <u>stomach</u>. The stomach stirs the food and mixes it with juices.

What is the important word in this paragraph? How do you know this word is important?

_____

The word <u>stomach</u> is underlined. <u>Underlining</u> is a way of calling attention to an important word.

Boldface Words

Read the next three paragraphs. On the first line after each paragraph write the important word. On the second line tell how you know that the word is important. Write either the word **boldface** or the word <u>underline</u>.

1. Much of North America once was covered by **forests.** Forests are places where many trees grow.

_____   _____

2. Beavers build **dams.** The dam holds back the flow of water in a stream. A pond is formed. Beavers then build their home in the pond.

_____   _____

3. Dogs have good eyesight. But they usually hunt by <u>scent</u>. Dogs are led by the scent, or smell, of the animal they are following.

_____   _____

Finding the Important Word

Read these short paragraphs. On the first line after each paragraph write the important word. On the second line write the meaning of the important word.

Some desert animals spend their days in a **burrow.** In this underground home they can stay cool.

_____

_____

Air covers the earth like a huge blanket. This blanket of air is called the **atmosphere.**

_____

_____

The pores, or tiny openings, in your skin let sweat escape. It is important to keep your skin clean. Then the pores can do their job.

_____

_____

During the short summer months the tundra **thaws.** When the ice melts, lakes and swamps form. Plants grow in soil that once was frozen.

_____

_____

Unit 1 | Environment and Ecology

Do you know how rare the bird in this photo is? The bird is a whooping crane. Only about two hundred of them are living today.

When pioneers moved to the West, there were many whooping cranes. They lived in Canada in the summer and in Texas during the winter. Then people changed the land. They cleared forests, drained swamps, and built cities. Chemicals that farmers used ruined much of the whooping crane's food, and hunters shot the birds. Little by little, they began to die out. By 1941, there were only 15 whooping cranes left.

Just in time, people started working hard to keep the whooping crane from disappearing. Laws were passed to protect them. Scientists studied whooping cranes to learn more about them.

Why is it important to save the whooping crane? Every animal and plant plays a part in the way nature works. If one kind of life dies out, it is a sign that the balance of nature has been upset. Another kind of life may die out, too. The whooping crane is only one of many animals and plants that scientists are trying to save.

The whooping crane is the largest crane of North America.

Chapter 1 | Deserts

The Great American Desert is a hot and dry place year round.

A What Are Deserts Like?

Wherever you live there are living things and non-living things around you. The things around you make up your **environment.** There are many different kinds of environments on the earth. A desert is one kind of environment.

A **desert** is a region, or place, in the world where there is very little rainfall. Most pictures you see of deserts show places covered with sand. In many places the sand has been shaped into **dunes,** or hills, by the wind, but deserts are mostly rock-covered. Even the great Sahara Desert in Africa is only one-tenth sand. The rest of the Sahara (90 percent) is rocky.

Most deserts are very hot during the day. Death Valley in the western United States is a hot desert. Some deserts are cold. A few cold deserts are found in the northwestern United States, but all deserts are alike in one important way. They are all very dry. A desert receives less than 25 centimeters of rainfall each year.

Objectives

A1 to describe what a desert is

A2 to identify different kinds of deserts

Check Up

A1 A desert is a place where there is _____ rainfall. All deserts are _____.

A2 Some deserts, like Death Valley, are very _____, but others are _____.

Most of a desert is _____-covered.

B Plants of the Desert

As you know, living things need water to stay alive and grow. To grow in a place with so little rainfall, plants must have special parts, or **adaptations.** Desert plants have special kinds of leaves, stems, and roots. These adaptations help them live through long, hot periods without water.

This part of the Great American Desert is in Arizona. The tall cactus plant is the saguaro, or giant cactus.

Many plants grow in the Great American Desert. This desert is in the southwestern United States. Most of the rain that falls on the Great American Desert falls during the spring. Then the desert plants bloom. Their brightly colored flowers last for only a few weeks. Then the flowers drop off. The plants almost stop growing.

Check Up

B1 Desert plants have _____

to help keep them alive.

B2 Rain falls in the Great American Desert mostly

during the _____.

The cactus plant has roots close to the surface of the ground. The roots spread out and soak up any water around the plant. After a rainfall a cactus plant looks fat because it stores water in its stem.

The mesquite plant has very deep roots. These roots grow 18 to 30 meters into the ground. There, the roots find water for the plant.

An **oasis** is a place in the desert where there is water. Usually, this water comes from a spring underground. In an oasis, palm trees and other plants can get the water they need to grow. Some deserts have many oases while others have very few.

Objectives

B3 to tell where the cactus stores water

B4 to name a desert plant with deep roots

B5 to locate where water is found in the desert

Check Up

B3 Water is stored in the _____ of the cactus.

B4 The roots of the _____ plant grow deep into the ground.

B5 A place in the desert where water is found is called an _____.

Discover for Yourself

How quickly does water evaporate from containers with different shapes?

Materials

- shallow baking pan
- glass measuring cup
- water
- clock

Procedure

1. Put 120 mL of water in the baking pan and 120 mL of water in the glass measuring cup. Leave the containers together and note the time.
2. Check the containers after an hour. Keep checking them every hour until the water has disappeared.

Results

1. How long was it until all the water had disappeared from

    the baking pan? _____ days _____ hours

    the measuring cup? _____ days _____ hours

2. Where did the water go? _____

_____

3. In which container did the water evaporate

sooner? _____

4. The amount of water that is exposed in a pan is like the amount of a desert plant that is exposed to the sun. We call this the "surface area" of the plant. From your experience with the two containers, do you think it would be better for a plant on the desert to have a big surface area like the shallow baking pan or a small surface area like the measuring cup? _____

The kangaroo rat has long, powerful hind legs. Can you see why it's called a kangaroo rat?

Dromedary camels have one hump. They are raised especially for riding and racing.

C Animals of the Desert

Animals that live in the desert also have special adaptations. The camel, for example, is called "The Ship of the Desert." The camel is adapted, or has special abilities, to live in a dry land. It can store a lot of water in its stomach. It can also store a lot of fat in its hump. The fat is "food" for the camel. Because of this a camel can go for many days without food or water.

The kangaroo rat is adapted to life in the American desert. It does not need fresh drinking water. It gets its water from the insects and seeds that it eats. It feeds at night. During the day it lives in its underground home called a **burrow.** There it keeps cool out of the sun.

Objectives

C1 to recognize where the camel stores its water and food

C2 to identify where the kangaroo rat gets its water

C3 to explain how the kangaroo rat keeps cool in the desert

Check Up

C1 The camel stores water in its _____ and

fat in its _____.

C2 The kangaroo rat gets its water from the

_____ and _____ it eats.

C3 In the daytime the kangaroo rat goes into a

_____ to keep cool.

Objectives

The sidewinder rattlesnake lives in our southwestern desert. It slides along the sand sideways. That is why it is called a sidewinder. Rattlesnakes are **reptiles.** A reptile's blood temperature is affected by its environment. If the sidewinder stayed in the desert sun, it would get very hot and die. So it rests during the day. It finds a shady place under a cactus or a rock. Sometimes it crawls into the burrow of another desert animal. At night the sidewinder comes out to feed on small animals. Its poisonous fangs kill very quickly. Then it swallows its victim whole.

The roadrunner is found in the southwestern deserts of the United States and Mexico. This bird would rather run than fly. It can run very fast. It feeds on small snakes and lizards. It moves so fast that the snake does not have a chance to strike. Like other desert animals the roadrunner needs little water. It gets its water from the food it eats.

Check Up

C4 The sidewinder rattlesnake gets its name from the fact that it moves _____.

C5 In the day the sidewinder rests under a _____, or a _____, or in a _____.

C6 The roadrunner would rather _____ than _____.

This sidewinder snake is in motion. You can see what kind of tracks it makes in the sand. On the right, the roadrunner races across the desert.

16

Discover for Yourself

How do camels travel on desert sand?

Materials

- shoe box
- sand
- 2 pencils
- piece of thick cardboard
- thumbtack

Procedure

1. Fill the shoe box about half full of sand.
2. Cut a piece of cardboard, 5 cm × 5 cm. Use the thumbtack to fasten the cardboard square onto the top of the eraser of one pencil.
3. Push the eraser end of the plain pencil into the sand. Now push the pencil with the cardboard on top of it into the sand.

Results

1. Which pencil was harder to push into the sand?

_____

2. The foot of the camel is very wide. It is flat and spreads out as the camel walks. How does this help it

walk on sand? _____

_____

_____

Chapter Summary

- The things around you make up your environment.
- A desert is an environment that has very little rainfall.
- Most deserts are hot, but a few are cold.
- Desert plants have special adaptations to help them live through periods without water.
- Desert plants bloom in the spring when the rains fall.
- Some desert plants have spreading roots or very deep roots to get water. Some plants can store a lot of water.
- An oasis is a place in the desert where there is water.
- Desert animals have special adaptations to help them live in a dry area.
- Some desert animals store food and water. Others get water from the food they eat.
- Many desert animals sleep during the day and feed at night.

This Sahel farmer is caring for his cattle.

Growth of a Desert

The largest desert in the world is the Sahara Desert in Africa. The Sahara is almost the size of the United States, but the Sahara is getting bigger. Scientists say it has spread more than 200 kilometers south in less than two years.

The area south of the Sahara is called the Sahel. Millions of people live in the Sahel. They farm the land and raise cows, sheep, and other animals. In some years the Sahel gets little or no rain. When there is not enough rainfall, the soil blows away. The farm land turns into desert.

In dry years there are not enough crops and animals to feed the people. So farmers cut trees to make more farm land. They raise more animals which eat all the grass. Without trees and grass to hold the soil, the desert keeps spreading, and people starve.

People have thought about different ways to slow the growth of the Sahara. One idea is to build areas to store grain. Farmers can then store extra crops from good years to be used in dry years. Trees could be planted to keep the soil from blowing away. Raising fewer animals and moving some people away from the Sahel would also slow the growth of the desert. Many of the people would not be happy about moving from their homeland, but steps must be taken soon to slow the growth of the Sahara.

Problem Solving

Life on the desert is very harsh. The desert is so dry and hot sometimes that most animals cannot live there at all. How do desert animals survive? How have they adapted to desert life?

If you had to spend a week in the desert, what would you do to survive?

Step 1 Make a problem solving plan. Discuss the question with the class. Make a list of animals that live in the desert.

Step 2 Gather information. Read about each animal in an encyclopedia or in library books.

Step 3 Organize your information. Make a chart like the one below.

	Animals	Light color	Dark color	Active during day	Active at night
1.					
2.					
3.					
4.					

Step 4 Analyze your information. What do desert animals have in common?

Step 5 Generalize. How do these common features help desert animals survive?

Step 6 Make a decision. As you have studied this problem, you have probably thought of ways to survive in the desert. What are they?

In each sentence there is a word missing. Look for the missing word in the list at the side of the page. Then, fill in the blank with the correct word.

1. The _____ plant has very deep roots.

2. Some desert animals live in a _____ underground.

3. The things around you make up your _____

4. The camel stores water in its _____.

5. A place that gets less than 25 centimeters of rain is called a _____.

6. An animal whose feet are adapted for walking in the sand is the _____.

7. In the desert, a place where there is water is called an _____.

8. The _____ stores water in its stem.

9. The camel can travel many kilometers using the food stored in its _____.

10. Small snakes are food for a fast bird called the_____.

environment
desert
mesquite
camel
hump
oasis
cactus
burrow
roadrunner
stomach

Circle the letter in front of the word that best completes the sentence.

1. An animal with a temperature that is affected by its surroundings is a _____.

(a) reptile
(b) rat
(c) roadrunner

2. A sidewinder is a kind of _____.

(a) bird
(b) rattlesnake
(c) deer

3. A kangaroo rat gets water from _____.

(a) lakes
(b) streams
(c) food

Chapter 2 | Forests

A Forest Layers

All forests are made up of different layers. Tall tree-tops make up the uppermost **canopy layer.** The tops of smaller trees make up the next layer called the **understory layer.** Below that is the **shrub layer.** It is made up of woody-stemmed bushes and shrubs that grow close to the ground. Still lower, flowers, grasses, mosses, and mushrooms make up the **herb layer.** Below the herb layer is the **forest floor.** It is made up of soil and dead leaves.

There are many different kinds of forests in the world. The kind of forest in an area depends on the area's climate and rainfall. **Climate** means the kind of weather a place has over a long period of time. For example, the climate around the equator is very hot and wet. So, forests in that area are different from forests in cooler, drier places.

Objectives

A1 to list what the layers of a forest are called

A2 to describe what the word climate means

A3 to tell why all forests are not the same

The fallen tree is lying on the forest floor. After a long time it will rot and become part of the forest floor.

Check Up

A1 The uppermost forest layer is called the

_____ layer. The tops of smaller trees make

up the _____ layer. Bushes and shrubs make

up the _____ layer. Flowers and grasses

make up the _____ layer.

A2 The kind of weather a place has over long periods

of time is called its _____.

A3 Forests are different from each other. This is

because of the _____ and _____ of

the places where they are found.

B Plants of the Rain Forest

Objectives

B1 to locate where most rain forests are found

B2 to recognize what the climate is like in most rain forests

B3 to explain why so little sunlight reaches the rain forest floor

B4 to describe how vines adapt to life in a rain forest

The plants you see in the rain forest are palm trees. Which forest layer are you looking at?

Rain forests are located in hot, moist climates. Most rain forests of the world are found near the equator. There the temperature is about the same all year long. This means that plants have a twelve-month growing season.

Trees in a rain forest can grow as tall as 55 meters. This high above the forest floor, the canopy layer spreads out. It is so thick that very little sunlight reaches the forest floor. Without sunlight plants cannot live, but those plants adapted to life in a rain forest can live with only a little sunlight.

Some plants curl and twine, or twist. These plants are called **vines.** Vines have roots in the ground. As a vine grows it twines around a tree until it reaches the top. There the vine grows leaves and flowers. Only at the canopy layer can a vine get enough sunlight to grow leaves. These leaves make food to keep the vine alive.

Check Up

B1 Most rain forests are near the _____.

B2 The climate there is _____ and

_____.

B3 The canopy layer of the rain forest keeps

_____from reaching the forest floor.

B4 Vines grow leaves and flowers at the tops of trees

by _____ and _____ around

them.

Many kinds of orchid plants do not root in the ground. The roots of these orchids cling, or hold on, to the side of a tree. The roots take water directly from the air. The orchid grows near the top of a tree. There it gets the sunlight it needs to live.

Trees do not grow close to the river banks in a rain forest. Therefore, sunlight can reach the ground near the river bank. Plants of the shrub and herb layers can grow there. Some of these plants grow very tall. For example, bamboo can grow up to 35 meters tall. Bamboo is a plant that belongs to the woody grass family.

Fungi are nongreen plants that cannot make their own food. Some fungi get their food by feeding on the remains of dead plants and animals. Other kinds of fungi feed on living things. Some fungi are so small you need a microscope to see them. Others, like the common mushroom, are larger and may weigh as much as half a kilogram.

Fungi are an important group of plants. Some fungi are harmful. They can spoil food and cause disease. Some fungi are poisonous and can make you very sick. Never eat unknown mushrooms you find growing in the woods. Other fungi help speed up the decay of dead plants. The dead plant matter goes back into the soil to make it richer. Certain fungi, like molds, can be helpful. Penicillin, for example, is taken from a mold. Penicillin is a drug that works against infection. It should never be taken without a doctor's advice.

Check Up

B5 The roots of the _____ plant that lives on the side of a tree get water from the _____.

B6 In the rain forest _____ do not grow close to the river. So _____ reaches the shrub and herb layer.

B7 The grass known as _____ can grow to be 35 meters tall.

B8 Fungi are _____ plants. They cannot make _____.

B9 Fungi speed up the decay of dead _____ and _____. Mold is a kind of fungus from which _____ is made.

B5 to tell about a plant that gets water from the air

B6 to explain why shrubs grow near river banks in rain forests

B7 to identify a grass that grows up to 35 meters tall

B8 to describe what fungi are

B9 to recognize why fungi are important plants

These tall plants are bamboo. This giant grass grows many branches.

Discover for Yourself

Why are fungi important to life on earth? What happens to food that isn't eaten?

Materials

- foods—bread, jam, cottage cheese, milk, fruit
- plastic margarine containers and lids

Procedure

1. Put some of each food into separate plastic bowls, place the lids on them, and then place all the bowls in an out-of-the-way part of the classroom.
2. Check the foods every day for two weeks.

Results

1. On a separate piece of paper draw each of the foods after one week and again after two weeks.

2. The fuzzy or thread-like growths on the foods are called molds. They are a type of fungi. There may also be yeast growths or even bacteria which will appear wet or waxy. Does there seem to be any yeast

or bacteria growing on your food? _____

_____

3. Do you think there is more than one kind of mold

growing on your foods? _____

What makes you think that? _____

_____

4. The molds are spoiling the food. Why is that

important to life on earth? _____

_____

C Animals of the Rain Forest

Animals in rain forests have adaptations that help them **survive,** or stay alive. The sloth, for example, has curved claws. This adaptation has helped the sloth live in the rain forest. This slow-moving animal uses its claws to hang from trees and to gather leaves, fruit, and nuts for food.

Monkeys have long arms and tails that have helped them adapt to life in the rain forest. These adaptations help the monkey move about and find food in the trees. The monkey swings from branch to branch using its long arms. Its long tail helps the monkey keep its balance.

Parrots and toucans are two kinds of birds that live in rain forests. These brightly colored birds have large, strong beaks. This adaptation helps them to crack the nuts and crush the fruit they eat.

Check Up

C1 The sloth's _____ allow it to hang from trees in the rain forest.

C2 Monkeys are able to move about and find food in the trees of the rain forest because of their _____ and _____.

C3 Parrots and toucans have strong _____ to crack nuts and crush fruits.

The long arms and tail of the monkey help it move quickly through the trees to find food. The beak of the parrot is made for cracking and crushing. Its feet are made for gripping trees.

25

Objectives

C4 to recognize how the anteater is adapted to life in a rain forest

C5 to explain how dead plants make room for living plants and animals

C6 to tell how the termite and earthworm aid in the process of decay

The anteater lives on the rain forest floor. This animal feeds on insects, and it has very sharp, strong claws. With these the anteater tears apart ant and termite nests. Its long, sticky tongue picks up the ants and termites.

The forest floor is filled with insects. It is also covered with dead plants and branches of trees. These dead plants must **decay,** or rot. Otherwise they would take up a lot of space. Soon there would be no space for living plants and animals. The termite is an insect that feeds on wood. The termite aids, or helps, in the decaying process of dead branches.

The earthworm also aids in the decaying process. Earthworms live in the soil. Waste from the food of the earthworm is left on the forest floor. The earthworm's waste helps rot dead plants.

Check Up

C4 The anteater has _____ which it uses to tear apart ant and termite nests.

C5 Dead plants _____ to make room for living plants and animals.

C6 The _____ eats dead wood on the forest floor. The _____ from earthworms helps rot dead plants.

Some termites live in wood and others live in soil. The termite on the right lives in soil. Earthworms live in soil in land areas all over the world.

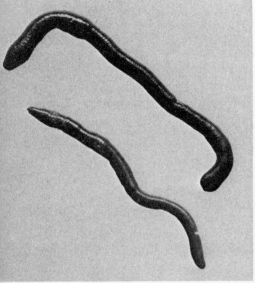

26

Discover for Yourself

How do earthworms help keep the soil loose?

Materials

- aquarium
- soil
- earthworms

Procedure

1. Put the soil in the aquarium, making sure it is packed down. Moisten the soil if it seems dry.

2. Put earthworms into the aquarium on top of the soil. Observe the earthworms for a few days.

Results

1. What did you see the earthworms do after a few

hours? _____

_____

2. After a few days, dig up the soil. What do you

notice? _____

_____

3. It is important for earthworms to loosen the soil. By tunneling through the packed soil, earthworms leave spaces in it. Plant roots and animals that live in the soil require the air that collects in these spaces. The spaces left by the worms also allow water to penetrate the soil when it rains. Water is important for all the plants that grow in the soil. What would happen

if there were no worms in the soil? _____

_____

_____

_____

This is an oak tree of the deciduous forest. It is very large, and its branches hang low to the ground.

D Plants of the North American Forests

There are two main kinds of forests in North America. One is called **deciduous.** Deciduous trees are adapted to live in a climate that has freezing weather part of the year.

Deciduous trees lose their leaves each fall. Each spring the trees grow new leaves. The leaves make food for the tree during spring and summer. With the coming of cold weather in the fall, the leaves drop. The sap stops flowing. The tree rests during the winter. In the spring the sap flows again, and the life cycle goes on.

Some deciduous trees, such as the maple and elm, have **seeds.** Others, such as the oak and hickory, have **nuts.** These are seeds within shells. The seeds and nuts fall to the ground. Some **sprout,** or grow, in the spring. Some of the sprouted seeds may even grow into trees.

Check Up

D1 Deciduous trees can grow in places where the climate is _____ part of the year.

D2 During the fall deciduous trees lose their _____ , and their _____ stops flowing.

D3 Four kinds of deciduous trees are _____, _____, _____ , and _____.

Objectives

D1 to name what kind of climate deciduous trees are adapted to

D2 to explain what happens to deciduous trees during the fall

D3 to list the names of four deciduous trees

The other kind of forest found in North America is the **coniferous** forest. The trees of this forest stay green all year long. In some places, deciduous trees are mixed with coniferous trees.

Coniferous trees have **cones.** The seeds of the trees are inside the cones. The leaves of these trees are called **needles.** Needles make the food for the tree.

Hemlock, spruce, and pine are coniferous trees. The redwood tree is another coniferous tree. Redwoods grow over 60 meters high. Some of them are over a thousand years old.

The shrub layer of North American forests can be thick. Many shrubs have berries which birds and other animals eat.

Check Up

D4 Coniferous trees are _____ all year round.

D5 The seeds of these trees are in _____.

Their leaves are called _____.

D6 Two kinds of coniferous trees are the

_____ and the _____.

D7 The shrub layer in North American forests can be

_____. Many shrubs have _____

which the forest animals eat.

The conifers on the left are members of the pine family. The giant sequoias of California are also known as Big Trees. Why do you think coniferous trees are called evergreens?

entire

serrate

lobed

pinnate

palmate

parallel

Discover for Yourself

How many different kinds of leaves are there?

Materials

- as many different leaves as you can find
- white paper
- peeled crayons

Procedure

1. Pick one leaf out of the collection. Lay it flat on the desk and cover it with a piece of paper. Now using the flat side of a crayon, rub across the paper, over the leaf. Bring out the pattern of the leaf.
2. Return that leaf to the pile and choose another that you know will make a different pattern. On a new piece of paper, make a crayon rubbing of this leaf.
3. Make at least five rubbings.

Results

1. Leaves can be simple or compound. There are several different kinds of compound leaves, but here is one example.

simple   compound

Label your leaves simple or compound.

2. All the edges of the leaves are different. They can be entire, serrate, or lobed.
Label any of your leaves that are entire, serrate, or lobed.

3. The veins on a leaf can be parallel, palmate, or pinnate.
Label your leaves parallel, palmate, or pinnate.

E Animals of the North American Forests

The black bear is one of the largest animals found in North America. It spends spring and summer feeding on almost every kind of food. It eats the berries that grow in the shrub layer of the forest. It eats small animals such as squirrels, frogs, chipmunks, and insects.

The black bear is adapted to the cold winter. All summer long it builds up a thick layer of fat. When cold weather comes, the bear sleeps most of the time in its **den.** Its den may be a cave. The layer of stored fat provides food for the bear. The black bear does not use much energy while sleeping. So it needs very little food.

The chipmunk is one of the small animals of the forest. During the summer it searches for seeds and nuts. It stores these in its burrow. It stays in the burrow during the winter. A lot of the time it sleeps, but the chipmunk wakes up now and then to eat.

Check Up

E1 In winter the black bear _____ most of

the time in its _____. The chipmunk

_____ most of the time in its _____.

A layer of

_____ provides the bear with

food. Stored _____ and _____

are the chipmunk's food in the winter.

Objective

E1 to explain how the black bear and chipmunk stay alive during winter in North American forests

Chipmunks are good at climbing trees. This is where they find much of their food.

The black bear is found in many national forests of North America. It is a large, meat-eating animal.

Objectives

E2 to list three ways the white-tailed deer is adapted to survive

E3 to tell how the woodpecker gets food

E4 to describe how the pill bug speeds up the decaying process

The top photo shows a mother woodpecker feeding her baby. At the right is a male white-tailed deer called a buck. Once deer were a source of food and clothing for native Americans.

The white-tailed deer has special adaptations that help it stay alive in the North American forests. The underside of the deer's tail is white. When there is danger the deer flicks up its tail. When the other deer see the flash of white, they run away. If a male deer is cornered, or trapped, by an enemy, it defends itself with its antlers, or horns. Baby deer are called fawns. Fawns are born with patches of white hair. When a fawn lies on the ground, it barely can be seen. The patches help it blend into its surroundings. This adaptation is called **protective coloration.** Because of its coloration the fawn is protected from enemies.

Woodpeckers of North American forests have strong, pointed beaks. This adaptation helps them get food. With its beak the woodpecker drills into the hard wood of trees. There, it finds the insects that it feeds on.

If you looked at some soil from a forest floor, you probably would find pill bugs. These bugs feed on decaying leaves and wood. This speeds up the decaying process on the forest floor.

Check Up

E2 The white-tailed deer flicks its _____ as a sign of danger. When cornered, the male deer uses its _____ to defend itself. Baby deer are protected from enemies by _____ .

E3 A _____ helps the woodpecker get food for survival.

E4 Pill bugs _____ on decaying leaves and wood.

Discover for Yourself

How do acorns grow into trees?

Materials

- styrofoam coffee cups
- potting soil with vermiculite
- acorns
- calendar
- ruler

Procedure

1. Collect acorns.

Acorns are produced by oak trees in the fall and can be planted any time after they ripen. The best time for planting, however, is in the early spring.

When you collect acorns, look especially in piles of damp leaves. In the spring you may find some acorns that are sprouting already. You may also find acorns that have been eaten by insects, so check your acorns for tiny insect holes.

2. Fill a styrofoam cup about halfway with the potting soil/vermiculite mixture. Now plant the acorn very close to the soil surface. Add a little water and leave the cup in a sunny place. Keep the soil damp over the weeks you observe the growth.

Results

1. The day you planted the acorn is "Day 1." Observe your acorn every day. What day is it when you first see the oak sprout? Check the calendar, and

count the days from "Day 1."_____

2. Once the acorn has sprouted, measure its height every day. Record the day number and its height for at least two weeks.

3. Now make a bar graph to show the results.

Chapter Summary

- Forests are made up of a canopy layer, an understory layer, a shrub layer, an herb layer, and the forest floor.
- Climate is the kind of weather a place has over a long period of time.
- Rain forests are found in hot, moist climates usually near the equator.
- Some rain forest plants twine around trees to get to sunlight. Others root on tree trunks.
- Fungi are nongreen plants that cannot make their own food.
- Rain forest animals are specially adapted to live in trees or on the rain forest floor.
- Dead plants on the forest floor decay and make space for living plants and animals. Fungi, insects, and earthworms help this process.
- North American forests are deciduous or coniferous. In some places they are mixed.
- Some North American forest animals adapt to life by sleeping during cold weather. Others have protective coloration.

Protectors of Our Parks

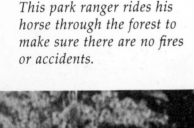

This park ranger rides his horse through the forest to make sure there are no fires or accidents.

Have you ever been to a public forest or park? If you have, you probably have seen a park ranger. Park rangers are the people who wear brown or green uniforms and hats like Smokey the Bear. They are there to help you and to keep the park safe.

A big part of a park ranger's job is to teach visitors about the plants and animals in the park. Park rangers also explain other parts of the environment such as rocks, hills, and streams. They teach the visitors by giving slide shows and tours. Many times they make displays that help explain the park.

Park rangers teach visitors about the parks because they want them to understand the environment of the park. They hope the people will treat the park with respect. Then other visitors who come to the park can enjoy the same natural beauty.

Park rangers also protect the park from dangers such as fire and harm from careless visitors. Sometimes rangers must help visitors in trouble. They find lost people, and when there has been an accident, they give first aid.

Park rangers may work in a city, near a city, or far away from any city. Park rangers spend most of their time outdoors. They must know a lot about plants, animals, and earth sciences to be good at their jobs.

Problem Solving

The tropical rain forest and the North American forest are two very different places in which to live. Animals that live in the rain forest have special characteristics to help them survive. They might not be able to survive in the North American forest.

If you were a wolf, would you rather live in the tropical rain forest or the North American forest?

Step 1 Make a problem solving plan. Discuss the question with the class.

Step 2 Gather information. Read about the wolf in an encyclopedia or in library books. Read more about tropical rain forests and North American forests.

Step 3 Organize your information. Make a list of the wolf's characteristics that would help it adapt to the rain forest, and a list of its characteristics that would help it adapt to the North American forest.

Step 4 Analyze your information. Which list is longer?

Step 5 Generalize. How do the characteristics in the longer list help the wolf to survive?

Step 6 Make a decision. Based on what you have studied, where would you want to live if you were a wolf?

In each sentence there is a word missing. Look for the missing word in the list at the side of the page. Then, fill in the blank with the correct word.

equator
termite
coniferous
canopy
deciduous
fawns
needles
fungi

1. Trees that lose their leaves in the winter are called

_____ trees.

2. Nongreen plants that feed on other plants and animals are called _____.

3. The top layer of a forest is the _____ layer.

4. Most of the rain forests of the world are found near the _____.

5. The _____ is an insect that feeds on dead wood.

6. Trees that have cones and stay green in the winter are called _____ trees.

7. Baby deer are called _____.

8. In North American forests most trees that stay green have leaves called _____.

Circle the letter in front of the word that best completes the sentence.

1. Plants that twine and curl around other plants to reach the light are called _____.

(a) trees
(b) flowers
(c) vines

2. The kind of weather a place has over a long period of time is called its _____.

(a) temperature
(b) climate
(c) rainfall

3. The animals and plants in a rain forest have special _____ that help them survive, or live there.

(a) adaptations
(b) layers
(c) burrows

Chapter 3 | Grasslands and Polar Regions

A flock of romney sheep feeds on the grasslands of New Zealand. Sheep can eat grass so close to its roots, that sometimes only soil is left.

A What Are Grasslands Like?

When you think of Africa do you think of jungles and rain forests? It may surprise you to know that over half of Africa is grassland. A large part of the United States is also grassland. It is known as the **prairie.**

Grasslands are areas that have between 50 and 65 centimeters of rainfall a year. This much rain would support a forest, but constant wind blows on grasslands and dries the topsoil. Only trees that can store water or have deep roots grow on grasslands.

The soil of grasslands is very rich. As grass dies and rots, it helps make the soil **fertile**, or rich. Then, other plants will grow better in the fertile soil.

Objectives

A1 to tell how much rain falls on grasslands

A2 to explain why soil of grasslands is rich

Check Up

A1 Grasslands get between _____ and

_____ centimeters of rain each year.

A2 As _____ dies and rots, it helps make

the soil rich.

B Animals of the Grassland

Most animals that live on grassland are plant eaters. Animals that eat only plants are called **herbivorous** animals. Meat-eating animals feed on the plant-eating animals. Meat-eating animals are called **carnivorous** animals.

One herbivorous animal of the grasslands of Africa is the zebra. Its teeth are adapted for eating plants. The zebra uses its sharp front teeth to bite off pieces of grass. Its flat back teeth mash the grass. The zebra runs very fast. It needs to run fast to get away from its enemies.

One of the zebra's enemies is the lion. The lion is a carnivorous animal. It feeds on zebras and other herbivorous animals. It uses its very sharp claws and teeth to kill and tear apart the animals it feeds on.

Locusts are a kind of grasshopper. Sometimes they **migrate,** or move, in a swarm. Then there are so many of them that the sky darkens. When they settle down in the grassland, they eat most of the plants. In this way they destroy the grassland.

Objectives

B1 to name the animals that feed on plants are called

B2 to tell what animals that feed on meat are called

B3 to describe how the zebra and lion are adapted to get food

B4 to identify the name of an insect that destroys the grassland

In the upper photo is the zebra. Its striped coat allows it to blend in with the plants of the grassland. Below, is the grasshopper which is found in grasslands all over the world.

Check Up

B1 Animals that feed on plants are called
_____ animals.

B2 Animals that feed on other animals are called
_____ animals.

B3 The zebra's _____ teeth are adapted for biting off grass. Its _____ teeth mash the grass. The lion uses its sharp _____ and _____ to get food.

B4 The _____ is an insect that destroys grassland.

38

Discover for Yourself

Where will grasses grow?

Materials

- five pans
- brick
- sponge
- soil
- calendar
- piece of clay
- paper towels
- water
- grass seed

Procedure

1. Fill one pan halfway with soil and moisten the soil with a little water.
2. Put the brick in another pan and fill that pan halfway with water.
3. Put the sponge in a pan and fill the pan halfway with water.
4. Roll a piece of clay into a ball and then make several indentations in the ball with your fingers. Wet the clay and put it in a pan.
5. Put a paper towel in the last pan and dampen it. Make sure there is not water standing in the bottom of this last pan.
6. Plant grass seed in each of these different environments. Sprinkle grass seed on the soil, the brick, and on the sponge. Put some grass seed in the indentations you made in the ball of clay and put grass seed on the damp towel.
7. Now put all the pans together and observe them everyday for about 10 days. Keep them moist.

Results

1. Record the day number that the grass sprouted on each surface. _____

2. Which grass looks most healthy? _____

3. How could you account for the differences in the way the grass grew? _____

C What Are the Polar Regions Like?

Objectives

C1 to explain where the polar regions are and what they are called

C2 to identify where the tundra is found

C3 to describe what the tundra is like in months of darkness and of light

The **polar regions** are areas around the North Pole and the South Pole. These regions have a very cold climate. Few plants and animals can live in such a climate. Each region has six months of daylight and six months of darkness. The polar region around the South Pole is called **Antarctica.** The polar region around the North Pole is called the **Arctic.**

Between the northern coniferous forests and the Arctic region is a plain called the **tundra.** During the dark months, the tundra is frozen. During the months of sunshine, parts of the tundra **thaw,** or melt. Lakes and swamps form. Ducks and other birds come to the lakes. Where there is soil, plants spring to life.

Check Up

C1 The polar region around the South Pole is called

_____. The region around the North Pole is

known as the _____.

C2 The tundra is found between the northern

_____ and the _____.

C3 In the months of darkness the tundra is

_____. In the months of light parts of the

tundra _____.

Caribou are able to live in rocky regions. Their hooves are sturdy, and help them to keep their balance. These caribou are able to walk along the edge of a very steep cliff.

This picture shows the beautiful wild flowers that grow in the Alpine Tundra.

D Plants of the Polar Regions

Algae, lichens, and mosses are simple plants that can grow in the polar regions. **Simple plants** do not have true roots, stems, or leaves. **Algae** are one of the most common forms of life. Most algae live in water. All algae can make their own food. They are sometimes used to make soil richer.

A **lichen** is made up of two parts: an alga and a fungus. The alga makes food for the fungus. The fungus protects the alga and keeps it moist. Some lichens live on trees. Others cling to rocks and help break them down. The remains of lichens help to make the soil richer.

A **moss** plant is tiny. Mosses grow on tree trunks and on rocks. They help break down the rock and make soil.

Very few trees grow on the tundra. Those that grow there do not grow upward. Because of winds and heavy snow, the trees grow along the ground. The trunks of the trees are very thin. This is due to the short growing season. Grasses grow along the southern edge of the tundra.

Objectives

D1 to list the names of three plants that grow in the polar regions

D2 to describe what a simple plant is

D3 to tell how trees grow in the tundra

Check Up

D1 Three plants that live in polar regions are

_____, _____, and _____.

D2 A simple plant does not have true _____,

_____, or _____.

D3 Trees of the tundra grow _____ the

ground. The _____ of the trees are thin.

41

Discover for Yourself

Where can you find lichens?

Materials

- different lichens
- magnifying lens
- white paper
- colored pencils or crayons

Procedure

1. Collect as many different lichens as you can. Although lichens are found in the polar regions, they are also found right around your own house. They can be found on trees, on rocks, even on buildings. They are frequently very flat plants, and they can be any color from gray and gray-green to bright yellow, orange, brown, or black.
2. Share them with the rest of the class.
3. Draw four different lichens on a piece of paper. Lichens are grouped in three major classes according to the way they grow: foliose, the leaflike lichens; fruticose, or shrubby lichens; and crustose, the crust-like lichens.
4. Label your lichen drawings according to growth type: foliose, fruticose, or crustose.

Results

1. Describe the places where you found your lichens.

2. Look at all the lichens in the class collection.

Describe the different colors.

3. Look at at least one lichen with a handlens and draw the way it looks when it is magnified.

E Animals of the Polar Regions

Animals that live in the polar regions have special adaptations to help them survive there. The penguin makes its home in Antarctica. This one-meter-tall bird is well adapted to life in a cold climate. The penguin has a layer of fat just under its skin, and there is a layer of feathers above the skin. This bird has short, strong wings, but it does not fly. The penguin uses its wings for swimming. Penguins feed on fish.

   The polar bear is well adapted for life in the Arctic. It has a layer of fat under its skin and white fur above. The color of its fur makes the polar bear hard to see. Why do you think this is so? The polar bear swims well. It feeds on seals, fish, and walrus from the cold waters of the Arctic.

   The snowshoe rabbit lives in the tundra. During the winter months its fur changes from brown to white. Then the rabbit's enemies cannot see it against the white snow.

Objectives

E1 to describe how the penguin is adapted for life in a cold climate

E2 to tell what the penguin uses its wings for

E3 to explain how the polar bear is adapted for life in a cold climate

E4 to recognize how the snowshoe rabbit hides from its enemies

Check Up

E1 A layer of _____ under its skin and a layer of _____ above protect the penguin from the cold.

E2 The penguin uses its wings for _____.

E3 The polar bear has a layer of _____ under its skin and _____ above to protect it from the cold.

E4 The _____ of the snowshoe rabbit turns from brown to _____ in the winter.

The snowshoe rabbit on the right can hardly be seen against the white snow. On the left, the polar bear lives amid the ice and snow.

Chapter Summary

- Grasslands get enough rain to support a forest. But constant wind dries the topsoil and prevents most trees from growing.
- The soil of grasslands is very rich.
- Animals can be herbivorous or carnivorous. Most animals that live on grasslands are herbivorous.
- Polar regions have a very cold climate. Few animals and plants can live there.
- The tundra is frozen during the dark months. It thaws partly during the months of sunshine, and many plants and animals live there then.
- Simple plants do not have true roots, stems, or leaves. Algae, lichens, and mosses are simple plants that grow in the polar regions.
- Animals in the polar region are adapted to life there by having such things as layers of fat under the skin and protective coloration.

Eyes on Antarctica

Antarctica surrounds the South Pole. It is a large land one-and-a-half times the size of the United States. But Antarctica is a cold, lonely place. In the winter, temperatures drop to minus 73°C. The summers are short and have cold temperatures, too. The snow and ice never melt completely. In some places, the snow is over 3 kilometers thick.

A scientist in Antarctica studies the killer whales living there.

Explorers did not go to Antarctica until 1820. Even now there are no real towns. There are stations where scientists live and study. Some things they have learned are causing much interest.

Scientists have found large beds of coal. They believe there is oil and natural gas. Useful metals such as iron, copper, nickel, and gold have been discovered. Other materials in Antarctica that could be useful are snow and ice. This is the world's largest supply of fresh water.

At this time, nothing is being taken from Antarctica. Because it is so cold, scientists have to find ways to get the materials. As these things become harder to find in other parts of the world, more eyes will be on Antarctica.

Problem Solving

Look at a globe of Earth. The equator is the imaginary line that separates the northern and southern hemispheres. In the northern hemisphere, the temperatures are cold and the days are short in December, January, and February. In June, July, and August the temperature is hot, and the days are long. What is the weather like in the southern hemisphere?

You are going to spend a week in the grasslands of northern Australia in December. What kinds of clothes will you pack? What if you were taking that trip in July?

Step 1 Make a problem solving plan. Discuss the questions with the class.

Step 2 Gather information. Read about the climate of Australia in an encyclopedia or library book. Find Australian grasslands on a map. Read about life in Australia.

Step 3 Organize your information. Write down what the weather would be like in each season.

Step 4 Analyze your information. What kinds of clothes would a person wear during each season?

Step 5 Generalize. Tell what the differences between Australia's and North America's seasons are.

Step 6 Make a decision. As you have gathered information on the climate of Australia, you have been thinking about the clothes you would pack if you had to spend a week there. What would you pack?

In each sentence there is a word missing. Look for the missing word in the list at the side of the page. Then, fill in the blank with the correct word.

carnivorous
tundra
mosses
lichen
polar bears
herbivorous
Antarctica
Algae
wings
zebra
locust
grasslands

1. _____ are one of the most common forms of life that usually live in water.

2. The _____ thaws during the months of sunshine in the polar regions.

3. Penguins use their short _____ for swimming.

4. White _____ hunt other animals near the North Pole.

5. The cold polar region near the South Pole is named _____.

6. The tiny plants that grow on rocks and help break them down are called _____.

7. Most animals that live on the grassland are _____ animals, or plant eaters.

8. Both lions and polar bears are _____ animals that feed on other animals.

9. A simple plant called a _____ is made up of an alga and a fungus.

10. The striped _____ of Africa feeds on grasses and other plants.

11. Areas that have between 50 and 65 centimeters of rain a year are known as _____.

12. A grassland animal that looks like a grasshopper and migrates in swarms is the _____.

Chapter 4 | Biomes

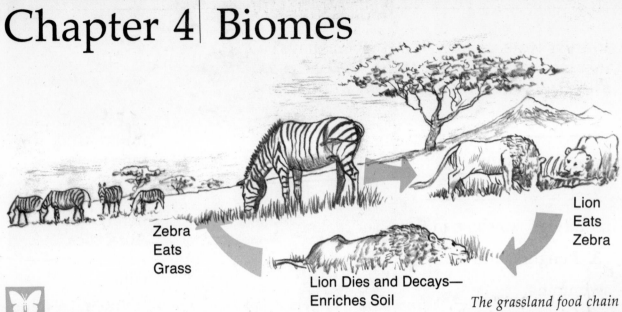

Zebra
Eats
Grass

Lion Dies and Decays—
Enriches Soil

Lion
Eats
Zebra

The grassland food chain shows the lion at the top. It is stronger than the zebra.

A Food Chains

A **biome** is an area that has a certain kind of climate. The desert, forest, grassland, and tundra are all examples of large biomes. Each biome is a home for certain plants and animals that have adapted to life there. The plants and animals depend upon each other for survival. The way they depend upon each other is shown in a **food chain.**

You read that green plants make, or produce, food. The herbivorous animals feed on the plants. The carnivorous animals eat the herbivorous animals.

When animals and plants die, their bodies decay and make the soil richer. New plants grow and make more food for more animals.

Every food chain begins with **producers,** or makers, and ends with **consumers,** or eaters. If a food chain is broken, life in a biome will change.

Objectives

A1 to explain what a biome is

A2 to describe what a food chain is

Check Up

A1 A biome is a large area with a certain kind of

_____. Plants and animals are _____

to life in a biome.

A2 A food chain shows how certain plants and

animals _____ on each other.

You cannot see the entrance and exit of this beaver lodge. They are underneath the water.

B The Beginning of a Pond Biome

Objectives

B1 to tell where pond biomes are found

B2 to explain how the beaver makes a pond biome

B3 to describe how the beaver is adapted for building lodges and dams

Large biomes have small biomes within them. A pond is an example of a small biome. A **pond** is a body of water that is usually smaller than a lake. Ponds usually are found in the larger forest biomes.

Some ponds are made by a small animal called a beaver. A beaver's home is called a **lodge.** Beavers live in lodges in the banks of a stream or river. They make their lodges out of branches, twigs, and mud. The lodges have two levels. The beavers live in the upper level. The entrances and an exit are below the water level. Sometimes the water level may not be high enough to cover the entrances and exit. Then the beavers make a dam of branches, mud, and stone. The dam blocks the flow of water in the stream. Water collects and forms a pond.

The beaver is adapted to pond life. It has long, sharp front teeth to cut trees and branches. With its flat tail it packs mud into the lodges and dams.

Check Up

B1 Small pond biomes are found in _____ which are larger biomes.

B2 Beavers make a pond when they build a _____ of branches and mud.

B3 Beavers have sharp _____ to cut branches. With their flat _____ they pack mud into the dams.

C The Growth of a Pond Biome

As the water in the pond behind a beaver dam rises, it spreads over land. The water floods the roots of many trees and smaller plants and they die. Dead trees become homes for thousands of insects. Soon woodpeckers come and drill holes into the trees looking for insects to eat. Wood ducks make their nests in large holes in the trees. A whole new food chain starts on the land around the pond.

Other forms of life grow in the pond. Reeds and cattails send roots into the mud. These plants grow above the pond's surface. Tiny duckweed plants float on the water.

Water bugs skim the pond's surface on tiny, hairlike legs. Insects such as mosquitoes and dragonflies lay their eggs on the surface of the pond.

Objectives

C1 to describe what happens to trees when a pond spreads

C2 to name three plants that grow in ponds

C3 to name two insects that lay eggs on a pond's surface

Check Up

C1 When a pond spreads out, the _____ of trees are flooded. The trees die and soon become homes for thousands of _____.

C2 Three kinds of plants in a pond are _____, _____, and _____.

C3 Two kinds of insects that lay eggs on a pond are _____ and _____.

The mallard ducks swimming in the pond make their nests in the tall grass. How many ducks do you see?

49

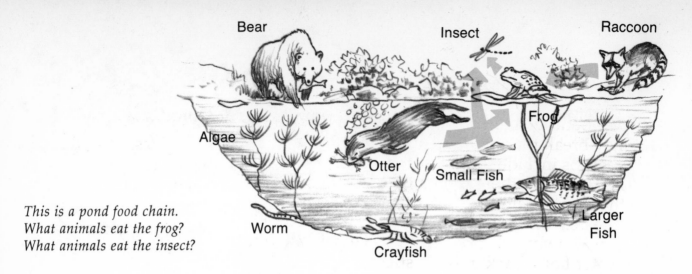

Bear　　　　Insect　　　　Raccoon

Algae

Frog

Otter　　Small Fish

Worm　　　　　　　　Larger
Fish
Crayfish

This is a pond food chain.
What animals eat the frog?
What animals eat the insect?

D　The Food Chain of a Pond Biome

A pond food chain begins with algae that grow in and near the water. As you know, algae are tiny green plants. Algae are producers because they make their own food. Algae are food for many fish. When algae die, they sink to the bottom of the pond. There they are eaten by worms, crayfish, and some kinds of smaller fish.

　Larger fish eat the smaller fish, worms, and crayfish. Both large and small fish feed on the insects that lay eggs on the pond. The frogs in the pond also feed on insects. The fish and frogs, in turn, are food for some of the mammals of the forest. Bears, raccoons, and otters, for example, eat fish.

Check Up

D1　Algae are called _____ because they can make their own food.

D2　Dead algae at the bottom of a pond are eaten by _____, _____, and _____. Larger _____ feed on the smaller _____. Fish and frogs eat _____. The fish and frogs are eaten by _____, _____, and _____.

Objectives

D1　to tell what algae are called and why

D2　to recognize how the food chain in a pond begins and ends

50

E The Death of a Pond Biome

A beaver pond biome dies when the dam breaks. The dam may break for a number of reasons. Some of these reasons include the following:

(1) As long as there is enough food, the beavers keep the dam in repair. When the food supply is gone, the beavers move to a new place and build a new dam. Slowly, the old dam breaks down, and the pond water flows back into the stream.

(2) After a heavy rain, the stream leading into the pond may flood. The dam may not be strong enough to hold the flood water. Then the dam breaks. Pond water rushes out.

(3) Sometimes the water behind the dam over-flows and floods roads or people's property. Then people tear down the dam. Some plants and animals in the pond die.

When a pond biome dries up, the forest biome begins to spread out again. Trees grow where cattails once grew. Moss covers the rocks. Grass grows. In a few years it becomes hard to tell that a pond was ever there.

Objectives

E1 to name three ways a pond biome may die
E2 to identify what happens when a pond biome dies

Check Up

E1 A pond biome dies if the beavers move away and do not repair the _____. Sometimes the stream leading to a pond floods and the _____ breaks. Sometimes _____ tear down the beaver's dam.

E2 When the pond biome dies, the _____ biome begins to spread out again.

The beaver has been collecting materials to build a dam. Notice the flat tail which is used to pack in the materials.

Discover for Yourself

What is a pond biome like?

Materials

- aquarium
- pebbles
- soil
- frog
- moss, ferns, or grass
- small plastic pan
- mealworms
- screening

Procedure

1. You can construct a model of a pond biome in your aquarium. Place the plastic pan in one corner of the aquarium, then put gravel around the pan. Cover the gravel with soil so that the edge of the pan is just above the top of the soil.

2. Fill the pan halfway with water and moisten the soil. Plant the moss, ferns, or grass in the soil.

3. Now the pond biome is ready for the frog. You may want to add a large rock for the frog to sit on. Place the screening tightly over the top of the aquarium.

4. Feed the frog mealworms. Observe your biome for several weeks. Keep the soil moist so that the plants do not die.

Results

1. On a separate sheet of paper keep track of how many mealworms the frog eats each day. If possible, make a bar graph using graph paper to show your results.

2. In what ways is your model the same or different from a real pond biome? _____

_____

_____

_____

Chapter Summary

- A biome is an area that has a certain kind of climate. The desert, forest, grassland, and tundra are all large biomes.
- A food chain shows how plants and animals in a biome depend on each other for survival.
- A food chain begins with producers and ends with consumers.
- Large biomes have small biomes within them, such as pond biomes within forest biomes.
- A pond biome can be started by beavers building a dam.
- A new food chain starts when trees and other plants are flooded out as a pond biome forms.
- A pond food chain begins with algae and ends with forest mammals.
- When a dam breaks, a pond biome dies.
- A forest biome spreads out again when a pond biome dies.

Did you know that a single drop of pond water can hold many living things? These tiny organisms are called plankton. Most plankton can be seen only with a microscope.

Some plankton just float through the water. They may be plants or plantlike. These produce their own food.

Other plankton are more like animals. They are able to move on their own in search of food. Some have "tails" that whip back and forth. Others have tiny "hairs" that help them swim. Still others look like tiny blobs of jelly. They slowly crawl on their way. One kind of plankton turns somersaults to move from place to place!

Even though plankton are very tiny, they are important. They are the first link in the food chain of a pond. The plantlike plankton produce their own food. They are eaten by many of the animal-like plankton. Both kinds of plankton are food for insects, tiny fish, and other small pond animals. The life of a pond depends on these unseen organisms.

This is what plankton look like under a microscope. They are the food source for larger plankton, insects, and fish.

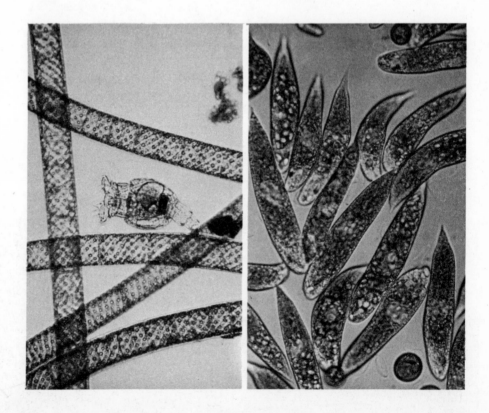

Problem Solving

Pretend that there is a swamp biome next to your house. In this biome, many kinds of animals exist. There are turtles, frogs, and fish, many kinds of birds, raccoons, and even a beaver. You enjoy watching the animals, but there is one problem. Swarms of mosquitoes live there, too. Someone has suggested spraying the swamp with chemicals that would kill all of the mosquitoes. Is this a good idea?

Step 1 Make a problem solving plan. Discuss the question with the class.

Step 2 Gather information. Read about how mosquitoes fit into the swamp food chain.

Step 3 Organize your information. List the animals that depend on the mosquitoes for survival.

Step 4 Analyze your information. How many of the animals in the swamp biome need the mosquitoes?

Step 5 Generalize. Are the mosquitoes necessary for the swamp biome to survive?

Step 6 Make a decision. As you have been thinking about the food chain of the swamp biome, you have probably decided whether using chemicals to destroy the mosquitoes is a good idea. Tell why or why not.

In each sentence there is a word missing. Look for the missing word in the list at the side of the page. Then, fill in the blank with the correct word.

1. Every food chain ends with _____.

2. Examples of large biomes are the desert, _____, grassland, and tundra.

3. Every food chain begins with _____.

4. A pond biome often begins with a _____ built by beavers.

5. Reeds and _____ send their roots into the mud of a pond.

6. The surface of a pond is used by _____ to lay their eggs.

7. A beaver _____ biome dies when the dam collapses.

forest
producers
dam
pond
mosquitoes
consumers
cattails

Circle the letter in front of the word that best completes each sentence.

1. Carnivorous animals feed on _____.

(a) plants
(b) animals
(c) seeds

2. In dead trees _____ drill for insects.

(a) wood ducks
(b) water bugs
(c) woodpeckers

3. Plants that float on the water are called _____.

(a) reeds
(b) duckweeds
(c) cattails

4. Beavers will stay in one place as long as there is enough _____.

(a) food
(b) mud
(c) branches

Chapter 5 | How People Change Biomes

A A Good Change

Do you think of a desert as being dry? Do you think of anything growing in a desert? You may be surprised to learn that many foods you eat are grown in deserts.

The soils of many desert biomes are rich, but without water, only desert plants can grow there. In some places, people have changed the desert biome. They have done this by bringing water to the desert. This process is called **irrigation.** In many places irrigation has changed dry land into rich soil.

Much farmland in the United States was once desert. It was changed by irrigation. Dams were built across streams to form lakes. Canals and ditches were built to carry water from the lakes to farms. In this way, crops get the water they need to grow. The Imperial Valley in California is an example of a desert that was turned into rich farmland through irrigation. In some areas, irrigation is done with water pumped from under the ground.

Irrigation must be done with care. It is possible to take too much water from streams and from underground supplies. This can cause problems for people living farther along the stream or in areas where the water is pumped out of the ground.

Objectives

A1 to describe how desert biomes have been changed

A2 to tell what irrigation is

In the irrigation of a bean crop you can see the water between the rows of plants. Slowly, it will sink into the ground to feed the roots.

Check Up

A1 Besides desert plants, other plants could grow in a desert if there was more _____.

A2 The process of bringing water to a desert is called

_____.

B A Bad Change

When settlers came to the prairies of the United States, they found thousands of buffalo. Prairie dogs lived in burrows under the thick soil. The settlers wanted to raise cattle and sheep. So they killed many of the prairie dogs and buffalo. Many more buffalo were killed for sport or for their hides by other people. The grazing cattle and sheep ate too close to the roots of the grass. Much of the grass died. Cattle and sheep owners had to buy food from farmers in order to feed their animals.

When the farmers came to the prairies, they cut through the grass to plant crops. They did not use good farming methods. They did not plant trees to break the strong winds that blow across the prairies. In the 1930's great winds blew over the prairies. Due to the winds and drought much of the rich farming soil blew away. The farmers could not grow crops. The cattle and sheep had nothing to feed on. A once rich area became a wasteland.

This is what happened to much of the grassland of the United States. Wind blew the soil into piles near the fence posts.

B Cattle and sheep ate the _____ down to its roots. Farmers did not plant trees on the prairies. So wind blew away the rich farming _____.

Discover for Yourself

What is sod?

Materials

- square of grass sod
- newspaper
- dull knife
- plain white paper and pencils

Procedure

1. Take a piece of sod and break it in half. Look at the roots of the grass. Try to separate one grass plant from all the rest.

2. A "cross-section" is a sideways view. Draw a picture of a cross-section of the sod.

Results

1. What was the first thing you noticed about the sod when you broke it apart? _____

_____

2. Are there any other plants growing in the sod besides the grass? _____

3. Why are there almost no other plants in the sod?

_____

_____

4. What holds the sod together? _____

_____

5. Are there any animals in the sod? _____

C Environment, Pollution, and Health

Objectives

C1 to describe what kinds of pollution harm the environment

C2 to explain what causes some kinds of pollution

C3 to recognize how pollution affects plants, animals, and people

Another way people change the environment is by putting harmful things into it. Putting harmful things into the environment is called **pollution.** Some things people do pollute the environment right away. Throwing cans, papers, or garbage in the city or country causes pollution quickly. Other things harm the environment more slowly. A factory may pour harmful wastes into a river. As poisons from the wastes build up, they can harm any living thing that uses the water.

Some of the most harmful kinds of pollution are air pollution, water pollution, and soil pollution. Many things cause these kinds of pollution. For example, **air pollution** can be caused by burning some kinds of coal. Some factories and power plants do this. Air pollution can also be caused by gasoline burned in the motors of cars, buses, and trucks. **Water pollution** can be caused by harmful wastes from farms, factories, and sewer systems. **Soil pollution** can be caused by chemicals that farmers use to kill insects and weeds.

This junkyard is an example of land pollution. Many citizens are cleaning up such areas in their cities.

The thick, black smoke from this smokestack contains dangerous chemicals that could be harmful to living things.

Plants, animals, and people are all harmed by pollution. Chemicals in water can kill plants and many kinds of animals, and can harm people. Air that is full of smoke and poisons can cause diseases of the lungs. Polluted soil can cause foods we eat to have harmful chemicals in them.

Check Up

C1 Some kinds of pollution are _____ pollution, _____ pollution, and _____ pollution.

C2 Air pollution can be caused by the burning of _____ and _____. Water pollution is caused by _____ from farms, factories, and sewers. Soil pollution is caused by _____ used to kill insects and weeds.

C3 Plants, animals, and people can all be harmed by _____.

D Protecting Plants and Animals

Objectives

D1 to tell what ecology means

D2 to explain what an ecological reserve is

Ecology is the study of living things in their environment. Plants and animals are adapted to live in certain biomes. The biomes may change. Then the plants and animals must change or move. If they cannot change or move, they will die. Dinosaurs once lived on the earth. Scientists think it is possible that the climate changed. The dinosaurs did not change. The dinosaurs did not move to another place. So the dinosaurs died.

An **ecological reserve** is a large area of land set apart for wildlife. Here plants and animals live undisturbed in their biomes. The living things on an ecological reserve are protected from the activities of people. People may visit some of the reserves, but they are not allowed to pick the plants. They are not allowed to hunt or even bother the animals. These reserves are found in all parts of the world.

Check Up

D1 The study of living things in their _____ is called ecology.

D2 An ecological reserve is a place where

_____ and _____ can live

undisturbed. In a reserve, living things are protected

from _____.

These African elephants are protected from hunters. They live safely in an ecological reserve.

62

E Ecological Reserves of the World

One very large ecological reserve is in Australia. The koala, a bear-like animal, is protected in that reserve. The duck-billed platypus also is protected in Australia. The platypus is a rare animal. This means that there are not many of them living. If the platypus were not protected, it could become **extinct.** This means that there would be none of these animals living on the earth.

The United States has many reserves. One is a buffalo reserve in the state of South Dakota. At one time thousands of buffalo, or American bison, lived on the Great Plains. Hunters killed the buffalo for their meat, skin, and bones. Buffalo almost became extinct. Now a few thousand buffalo live on the reserve in South Dakota. People can look at these buffalo and can take pictures, but they cannot kill the buffalo.

At one time millions of different animals lived on the plains, or grasslands, in Africa. Hunters came to the plains to kill elephants for their ivory tusks. Cities, towns, and farms were built on the plains. The animals were pushed out of their biomes. Plants, their main source of food, were destroyed. The animals of the African plains began to die out. Some people realized that soon many of the animals would be extinct. So they set up ecological reserves. One such reserve is the Kruger National Park in South Africa. The elephant and other animals are protected on this reserve.

Objectives

E1 to list the names of the animals protected in Australia

E2 to explain what extinct means

E3 to tell what happened to the American bison

E4 to describe how some animals are protected in Africa

Wallabies are smaller than kangaroos. They also are natives of Australia.

Check Up

E1 The _____ and the _____ are two animals that are protected in Australia.

E2 If an animal is _____ it means that none of its kind is living.

E3 The American bison was killed for _____, _____, and _____.

E4 One of the animals protected in Africa is the _____.

Chapter Summary

- People have changed desert biomes into rich soil by irrigation.
- People have harmed grassland biomes by poor grazing and farming methods.
- Air, water, and soil pollution are caused when harmful things are put into the environment.
- Pollution can harm all living things.
- Ecology is the study of living things in their environment, or biome.
- When biomes change, plants and animals must adapt or move or they will die.
- An ecological reserve is a large area set aside so that wildlife can live undisturbed.
- Ecological reserves are found all over the world.
- Ecological reserves protect some animals against becoming extinct.

Humans and the Manatee

The manatee, or sea cow, is a large, shy, gentle animal like a seal. The West Indian manatee lives in small family groups of about 15 members. They are found in the warm, shallow waters of Florida. Baby manatees are born live. Their mothers feed them milk until they are big enough to eat water plants by themselves.

There used to be many manatees in Florida. Now there are only about 1,000. Manatees were once hunted for food. But laws were passed to stop this.

This friendly manatee looks as though it is waving and speaking.

64

However, humans are still the manatee's worst enemy. People drive their motorboats where manatees live. The animals are too slow to get out of the way. About 100 manatees are killed each year by accidents with boats. People also ruin the manatees' biome. They drain the shallow waters to build houses, and sometimes they pollute the water. Without food and a safe home, the manatees die.

Many people want to save the manatee. Laws have been passed to keep boat traffic away from where the manatees live. Certain places called sanctuaries are set aside where people cannot ruin the environment. Scientists have taken some manatees to special tanks. Here they study them and feed them good food. This special care has helped sea cows have new babies. When the babies are old enough, they are put back in their natural home. If these new steps work, there may someday be many manatees again.

Problem Solving

Animals become extinct when human beings kill too many of them, or when their biomes change. If animals cannot adapt to changes in their biomes, they must find a new biome or they will die.

Suppose that the whooping crane's biome has changed, and you must create a new home for it. What kinds of things would you include in the new biome to make sure the whooping cranes survive?

Step 1 Make a problem solving plan. Discuss the question with the class.

Step 2 Gather information. Read about the whooping crane in an encyclopedia or library book.

Step 3 Organize your information. List the conditions that must exist in the whooping crane's biome. Include food, climate, and nesting areas.

Step 4 Analyze your information. Which conditions are most important for the whooping crane's survival?

Step 5 Generalize. Tell why these conditions are so important.

Step 6 Make a decision. What would your biome be like?

In each sentence there is a word missing. Look for the missing word in the list at the side of the page. Then, fill in the blank with the correct word.

ecology
irrigation
wasteland
extinct
pollution
sheep
buffalo
canals
reserves
soil

1. Putting harmful things into the environment causes _____.

2. Bringing water from one place to another in ditches is called _____.

3. Some countries have set up _____ where plants and animals are not disturbed by people.

4. When good soil is used up or blown away rich land can become a _____.

5. The study of living things and their environment is called _____.

6. Thousands of _____ once lived on the grasslands of the United States.

7. An _____ plant or animal is one that no longer lives.

8. Rich farming _____ is needed for plants to grow well.

Circle the letter in front of the word that best completes the sentence.

1. _____ pollution can be caused by burning coal and gasoline.

(a) Water
(b) Air
(c) Soil

2. The _____ did not change or move and became extinct.

(a) platypus
(b) koala
(c) dinosaur

3. Pollution can _____ all living things.

(a) make
(b) help
(c) harm

Understanding Pictures and Captions

This book has many pictures. Often the pictures have captions. The words under, above, or alongside of a picture are called the **caption.**

What information do you get from a picture and a caption? A picture is used to help you understand what you are reading. A caption is used to help you understand the picture.

Look at the picture below. What do you see in the picture?

Now read the caption below the picture. Does the caption help you to understand the picture better? Can you tell what the picture is about without reading the caption?

The water skier in this photograph is trying out some new equipment. He is testing the safety, strength, and comfort of a new type of binding. The binding binds, or holds, the skier's foot to the ski.

Captions That Ask a Question

Sometimes a caption is in the form of a question. Then you have to study the picture in order to answer the question.

Look at the picture of the boat. Read the caption.

Can you answer the caption question? If you cannot, then try these questions first: What kind of boat is shown? How many masts does the boat have? How many sails does it have? Now try answering the question in the caption.

How does this boat move through the water?

A macaw's beak is strong enough to crush fruit. A macaw belongs to the parrot family.

Sometimes the caption is on the side of the picture. Read the caption of the picture above. Then answer the questions about this picture.

Do all macaws look the same? _____

How are macaws alike? _____

_____

How does a macaw use its beak? _____

_____

Look at the picture below. Read the caption. Then answer the questions about the picture and its caption.

What are large groups of fish called? _____

Why do fish travel this way? _____

Tuna travel in large groups called schools. Traveling like this helps protect the tuna from enemies.

Unit 2 | Your Senses

Have you ever thought about how your brain helps you enjoy dinner? First your nose lets you know that dinner is almost ready. You *smell* the food being prepared. When someone calls you to dinner, you *hear* that it is time to eat. As you sit down at the table, you *see* the colors and shapes of the food. Then you might touch your plate or bowl to *feel* if it is hot or cold. The best part is when you take the first bite. You *taste* the food.

It is your brain that allows you to smell, hear, see, feel, and taste. Special sense organs on the outside of your body send messages to your brain. These messages tell your brain what your nose is smelling, your ears are hearing, or your eyes are seeing. Your brain lets you know about all the things happening around you all the time—not just at dinner time.

Chapter 6 | Sight

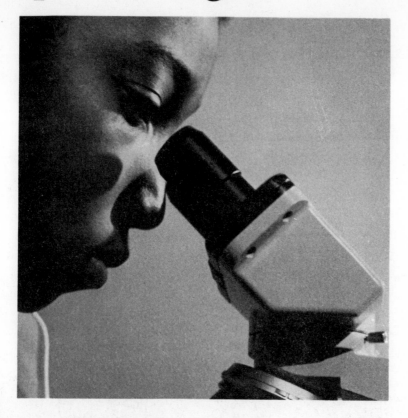

The microscope helps us see things that are too small to be seen by our eyes alone.

A Your Brain and Your Senses

You have five **senses:** sight, hearing, touch, taste, and smell. Each sense has a special **sense organ.** For example, your eyes are the sense organs for sight. **Nerves** connect the sense organs to the brain. The nerves carry messages to the brain. The brain decides what to do.

Here is an example of how your senses work. A car is coming at you. Your eyes see it. They send that message to the brain. Your brain thinks "danger." It quickly sends a message to your leg muscles. You jump out of the way.

Objectives

A1 to list the names of your five senses

A2 to identify how your sense organs are connected to your brain

Check Up

A1 The names of your five senses are _____,

_____, _____, _____, and

_____.

A2 Your sense organs are connected to your brain by

_____.

B How Your Eyes Are Protected

Your **eyes** are an important sense organ. You use your eyes to read the words in this book. You use your eyes to play games. Your eyes let you enjoy the beauty of a sunset or a smile.

Feel your face just above and below your eyes. Do you feel the hard parts around your eyes? These bones form a wall around your eyes. They keep large objects from striking your eyes. **Eyelashes** grow on your upper and lower eyelids. They keep tiny objects from getting into your eyes.

You blink your eyes about 25 times every minute. Each time you blink, your eyes are covered by a salty liquid called **tears.** They help wash tiny pieces of dust and dirt from your eyes.

Check Up

B1 The _____ in your face form a wall to keep large objects from hitting your eyes. Your _____ keep tiny objects out of your eyes.

B2 Tears wash out pieces of _____ and _____ from your eyes.

Objectives

B1 to recognize how bones and eyelashes protect your eyes

B2 to tell how tears protect your eyes

This closeup of the human eye shows the eyelashes. They protect the eyes from bits of dust and dirt that fly through the air.

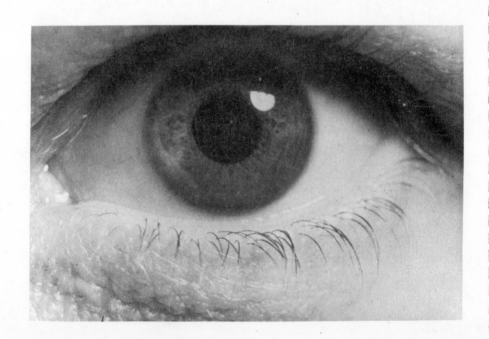

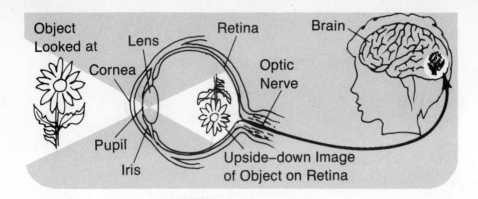

Object Looked at
Lens
Cornea
Retina
Brain
Optic Nerve
Pupil
Iris
Upside–down Image of Object on Retina

C How You See

Light enters the eye through the **cornea.** The cornea is a clear covering over the front of your eye. Then the light passes through the **pupil.** This is the round opening in the center of your eye. Surrounding the pupil is the **iris.** The iris is the colored part of your eye. It has muscles that control the amount of light that enters your eye.

After passing through the pupil, the light passes through the **lens.** The lens focuses the light, or brings it to a point, on the retina. The **retina** is the lining of the back part of the eyeball.

The **image,** or picture, of what you see is upside-down on the retina. This upside-down message is sent from the retina to the brain along the **optic nerve.** The brain turns the image right side up.

Objectives

C1 to list what parts of the eye light passes through

C2 to name what part of the eye controls the amount of light entering it

C3 to tell what part of the eye focuses the image on the retina

C4 to recognize what nerve sends the image to the brain

Check Up

C1 Light enters the eye through the _____,

passes through the _____ and then the

_____.

C2 The _____ controls the amount of light

entering the eye.

C3 The _____ focuses the image on the

_____.

C4 The _____ nerve sends the image to the

brain.

Discover for Yourself

How do your eyes play tricks on you?

Materials

- ruler

Procedure

1. Look at the drawings below.
2. Answer the question for each drawing *without* using your ruler.
3. Look at the drawings again. This time use your ruler before you answer the questions.

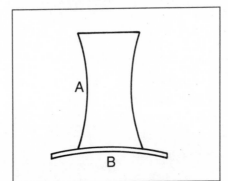

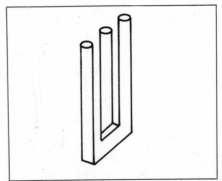

Which line is longer - line A or line B?

Look at this drawing Could you make this object?

Which boy is tallest?

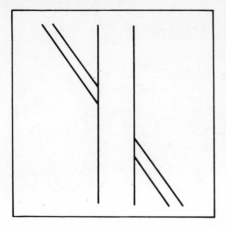 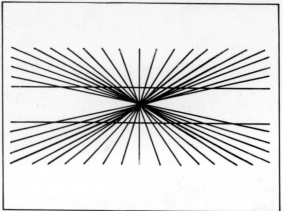

Are the lines straight
or bent? _____

Are the lines straight
or curved? _____

Results

1. Were your answers the same with and without the

ruler? _____

2. Which answer was correct—when you used the

ruler or when you did not use the ruler? _____

3. How did the ruler help you see the drawings bet-

ter? _____

D Taking Care of Your Eyes

Objectives

D1 to explain how bright light can hurt your eyes

D2 to describe how the eyes wash themselves

D3 to identify what some people wear to see better

D4 to tell why some workers wear goggles

Your eyes are very valuable. Most of what you learn about the world is learned through sight. It is important that you take good care of your eyes.

Bright light can injure, or hurt, the nerve endings in the retina. Never look directly at the sun. Protect your eyes from glaring sunlight. Some people wear dark glasses. Others wear caps or hats that shade their eyes.

Be careful when you read or write. Make sure the light does not shine in your eyes. The light should shine on the book or paper you are reading.

Once in a while, you may get a speck of dirt in your eye. Do not rub your eye. The speck of dirt could scratch the cornea. If your tears do not wash it out, you can use a special eyewash.

Eyeglasses help some people see better. If you have trouble seeing or you feel dizzy, you may need eyeglasses. An eye doctor can examine your eyes and let you know.

Some people must wear special glasses to protect their eyes. These glasses are called **goggles.** Workers who sand down wood wear goggles to keep wood dust out of their eyes. Can you think of other workers who should wear goggles?

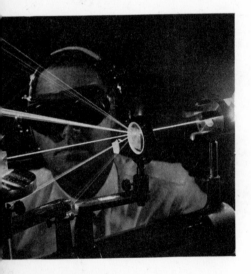

This scientist is working with laser beams. The goggles he wears protect his eyes from danger.

D1 Bright light may injure the nerve endings in the _____.

D2 The dirt that gets in your eyes is usually washed out by _____.

D3 Some people wear _____ to help them see better.

D4 Some workers wear goggles to _____ their eyes.

Discover for Yourself

How does a magnifying glass help you see details?

Materials

- magnifying glass
- newspaper or magazine pictures

Procedure

1. Choose a picture from a newspaper or magazine.
2. Look closely at the picture without using the magnifying glass.
3. Now look at the picture using the magnifying glass.

Results

1. What was the smallest thing you could see the first time you looked at the picture? _____

_____

2. What was the smallest thing you could see when you used the magnifying glass to look at the picture?

_____

3. Tell what forms the picture. _____

Chapter Summary

- The five senses are sight, hearing, touch, taste, and smell.
- Nerves carry messages from the sense organs to the brain.
- Eyes are sense organs that allow sight.
- Bones around your eyes, and your eyelashes and tears help protect your eyes.
- Light forms an image on the inside of the eye. This message is sent to the brain along the optic nerve.
- Eyes can be hurt by bright light or by specks of dirt that scratch the cornea.
- Eyeglasses help some people see better. Special goggles protect eyes in some workplaces.

A Reading Problem

This teacher is helping a student with reading by using flashcards.

David is a bright boy. He does well in art class and he has many friends, but David worries when it is time for reading. Sometimes he mixes *p* up with *q*. Sometimes the word *was* looks like *saw* to him. Sometimes a word looks upside down. Most of his classmates do not seem to make these mistakes. When David is asked to spell a word in class, some students may laugh. His teacher may get upset with him, but everyone needs to understand that David has a reading problem. It is called dyslexia.

Most people with dyslexia are bright. Yet they have trouble with reading, writing, and spelling. Their brains mix up the messages from their eyes. For example, their eyes may see the word *OIL*, but their brains "tell" them it is the number *710*. Scientists now think some people are born with dyslexia. They think certain parts of the brain grow differently before birth. So dyslexia is not a kind of brain damage. It is a difference in growth that causes reading problems.

Doctors do not know how to change those different parts of the brain to make reading easier, but they can train those with dyslexia to read better. Special ways to "un-mix" the words are taught. This training can help people with dyslexia read like everybody else.

Problem Solving

We depend on our sense of sight more than on any other sense. Without your sense of sight, you would do things differently.

Imagine what it would be like to wear a blindfold for a day. How would you have to change your routine to get ready for school in the morning? How would you use your senses to guide you?

Step 1 Make a problem solving plan. Discuss the question with the class.

Step 2 Gather information. List the things you do each morning to get ready for school.

Step 3 Organize your information. What senses are needed to complete each task?

Step 4 Analyze your information. Which tasks require sight?

Step 5 Generalize. How important is the sense of sight in your daily routine?

Step 6 Make a decision. As you have thought about what senses you use every day, you have probably decided what you would do differently to get ready for school if you were blind. What would you do?

In each sentence there is a word missing. Look for the missing word in the list at the side of the page. Then, fill in the blank with the correct word.

1. The _____ around your eyes keep large objects from striking your eyes.

2. Nerves carry messages from your sense organs to your _____.

3. Some workers wear _____ to protect their eyes.

4. The salty liquid called _____ helps wash your eyes.

5. The picture on the retina of the eye is _____.

6. Tiny hairs called _____ help keep dust out of your eyes.

7. You blink your eyes about 25 times a _____

brain
tears
goggles
upside-down
eyelashes
bones
minute

Circle the letter in front of the word that best completes the sentence.

1. The optic nerve carries messages from your _____ to your brain.

(a) ears
(b) nose
(c) eyes

2. Nerve endings in the _____ may be injured by looking at the sun.

(a) cornea
(b) lens
(c) retina

3. The amount of light that enters your eye is controlled by the _____.

(a) pupil
(b) iris
(c) cornea

4. The lens of the eye focuses light on the _____.

(a) cornea
(b) pupil
(c) retina

Chapter 7 | Hearing

A How Sound Is Made

Your sense of hearing gives you pleasure. It also warns you of danger, and it does much more for you. How many different sounds do you hear in a day? It would be almost impossible to count them. Have you ever thought about how sound is made?

Objective

A to describe what happens when an object vibrates

A sound engineer works with special equipment in a recording studio.

Discover for Yourself

How is sound made?

Materials

- tuning fork

Procedure

1. Tap the tuning fork gently against the side of a desk. Bring the tuning fork close to your ear.
2. Tap the tuning fork again. This time touch the tuning fork with your finger.

Results

1. What did you hear after you tapped the tuning

fork and placed it close to your ear? _____

_____

2. What did you feel when you tapped the tuning

fork and touched it with your finger? _____

When you hit the tuning fork against the desk, the ends of the tuning fork moved back and forth very fast. This back and forth movement is called **vibration. Sound** is made when an object vibrates.

Check Up

A When an object _____ it makes sound.

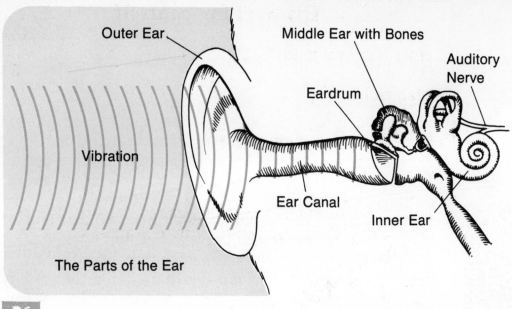

The Parts of the Ear

B How You Hear

Your **ear** is the sense organ for **hearing.** When an object vibrates in air, it makes the air travel in waves away from it. These waves are picked up by your **outer ear.** Your outer ear leads the sound waves into a little tunnel. This tunnel, part of the outer ear, is called the **ear canal.**

Sound waves travel through the ear canal and strike the **eardrum.** The eardrum, part of the outer ear, vibrates. As it vibrates, three tiny bones move in the **middle ear.** These bones send vibrations to the **inner ear.** Nerve endings in the inner ear pick up the vibrating message. They send it along the **auditory nerve** to the brain. The brain picks up the message as sound.

Objectives

B1 to tell what part of the ear picks up sound

B2 to describe how sound travels through the parts of the ear

B3 to recognize how the sound message gets to the brain

Check Up

B1 Sound waves are picked up by the _____.

B2 Sound then travels through the canal and hits the

_____. This part vibrates and moves three

tiny _____ in the middle ear. The middle ear

sends vibrations to the _____.

B3 Sound messages are carried to the brain along the

_____ _____.

Discover for Yourself

How does the outer ear help you hear?

Materials

- friend or classmate
- musical triangle

Procedure

1. Stand about three meters away from your friend. Have your friend tap the triangle lightly.
2. Push your outer ears flat against the side of your head. Have your friend tap the triangle lightly.
3. Cup your hands behind your outer ears. Have your friend tap the triangle lightly.

Results

1. When did you hear the sound of the triangle

loudest? _____

2. Why? _____

3. When was the sound of the triangle softest?

_____

4. Why? _____

5. How do your outer ears help you hear better?

Discover for Yourself

How do vocal cords feel when a person hums or speaks?

Materials

- partner

Procedure

1. Stand or sit facing your partner.

2. Put your fingers on your partner's throat under the chin. Your partner should talk or hum, sometimes loud and sometimes soft; sometimes high and sometimes low.

3. Do step 2 again with your partner's fingers on your throat.

Results

1. What did you feel when your partner talked or

hummed? _____

_____

2. Did it feel different when the sounds were loud

and soft, and high and low? _____

3. Which sound was the easiest to feel? _____

_____

4. Which sound was the most difficult to feel? _____

_____

5. You cannot feel sound. What did you feel as your

partner talked or hummed? _____

_____

C Pleasant and Unpleasant Sounds

Objectives

C1 to recognize why you have two ears

C2 to identify what kind of sound waves make pleasant sounds

C3 to describe what kind of sound waves make noise

Do you know why you have two ears instead of one? Two ears help tell where a sound is coming from. They also help you know how far away a sound is. Sound may reach one ear a little before it reaches the other. This difference tells your brain where the sound is coming from.

Some sound waves that reach your ears are regular and not too loud. These sound waves are pleasant. Musical instruments make pleasant sounds.

When sound waves are very loud or come from different directions they are mixed up. These sound waves are usually unpleasant. Sound waves that are too loud and too mixed up make noise. **Noise** is an unpleasant or unwanted sound.

Check Up

C1 Your two ears tell you _____ a sound is coming from and how _____ it is.

C2 Waves that are _____ and not _____ make pleasant sounds.

C3 Sound waves that are too loud and too unpleasant make _____.

Your sense of hearing gives you pleasure. Would it be pleasant to hear the sounds made by this marching band?

D Taking Care of Your Ears

You have been out on a cold winter's day. Which part of you usually gets cold first? It is probably your ears. If you spend much time in the cold air, you should protect your ears with a hood, hat, or earmuffs.

There is an old saying: "Never put anything smaller than your elbow in your ear." This is a good saying to remember. Your ear canal leads to the eardrum. The eardrum is very thin. Putting pencils or sticks in your ear could break the eardrum. This could cause a serious hearing problem.

Be sure to wash your outer ears. This not only keeps them looking better, but also keeps them free from dirt and germs.

Loud noises can be harmful to your ears. If you are around loud noises a long time, you may lose some of your hearing. Loud music is one example of a noise that can hurt your hearing.

Objectives

D1 to tell what to do for your ears in the cold weather

D2 to recognize how pencils or sticks can hurt your ear

D3 to explain why washing your ears is important

D4 to demonstrate how loud noises can harm your ears

Check Up

D1 If you spend time in the cold air, you should _____ your ears with a hood, hat, or earmuffs.

D2 You should never put a pencil or stick in your ear because you may injure your _____.

D3 Washing your ears helps to keep _____ and _____ out of your ears.

D4 Loud noises can cause you to lose some of your _____.

Construction workers must wear special headphones to protect the tiny bones and eardrums of their ears. Have you ever heard the noise from a jackhammer?

Chapter Summary

- Your sense of hearing can give you pleasure and also warn you of danger.
- Sound is made when an object vibrates.
- Your ear is the sense organ for hearing.
- The outer ear helps bring sounds to the other parts of your ear.
- Vibrating messages are sent from the ear along the auditory nerve to the brain.
- Having two ears helps you tell where a sound is coming from and how far away a sound is from you.
- Sound waves that are regular and not too loud make pleasant sounds. Unpleasant and unwanted sounds are noise.
- Loud noises can cause hearing loss.

The Electronic Ear

At the right is a picture of Dr. House's electronic ear. You can see its size compared to the quarter in the picture. The drawing below shows how a person would wear the electronic ear.

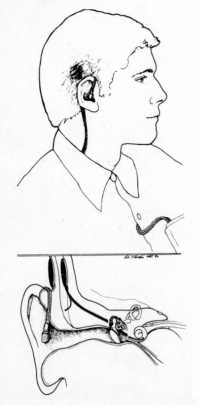

Deaf people are not able to hear because some part of their ear does not work properly. Now more than 200,000 deaf people in the United States may have some hope of hearing. Dr. William House of the House Ear Institute in Los Angeles, California, has made an electronic ear.

A tiny microphone worn near the ear picks up sound. The sounds are sent to a small computer that can be carried in a pocket or worn on a belt. The computer changes sounds into special messages.

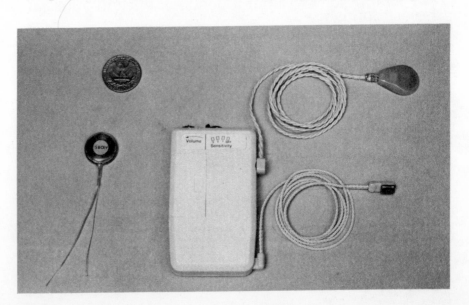

These messages are sent back to the ear. In the ear, they are picked up by the auditory nerve and sent to the brain.

The electronic ear will make it possible for some deaf people to hear sounds. Voices would not sound clear, but sounds like car horns and doorbells could be heard.

How will this invention help deaf people?

Problem Solving

Bottle-nosed dolphins are some of the most intelligent animals because they can communicate. They bark, and make clicking and whistling sounds. They even imitate human speech. Dolphins have a special talent called echolocation. They use this ability to find objects lost under water.

Can you guess how echolocation works? What underwater noises might interfere with echolocation? How can the dolphin help human beings by using echolocation?

Step 1 Make a problem solving plan. Discuss the questions with the class.

Step 2 Gather information. Read about dolphins and about echolocation.

Step 3 Organize your information. The word echolocation is made of two words. If you separate them, can you tell what the word means? Look it up in the dictionary.

Step 4 Analyze your information. Tell how echolocation is used.

Step 5 Generalize. Is echolocation a useful tool for human beings?

Step 6 Make a decision. As you have learned about dolphins and their talent for echolocation, you have probably thought of ways that dolphins can help human beings. What are they?

In each sentence there is a word missing. Look for the missing word in the list at the side of the page. Then, fill in the blank with the correct word.

1. Putting sharp things in your ear could break

the _____.

2. Sound waves that are mixed up make sound called _____.

3. Two ears help tell you where _____ is coming from.

4. Pleasant sounds are made by _____ sound waves.

5. Hearing can give you pleasure and warn you

of _____.

6. The _____ has three tiny bones.

eardrum
sound
regular
noise
middle ear
danger

Circle the letter in front of the word that best completes the sentence.

1. Washing your ears will help keep _____ out.

(a) germs
(b) sticks
(c) air

2. Your middle ear sends vibrations to your _____.

(a) brain
(b) inner ear
(c) eardrum

3. The ear canal is a _____ that leads from your outer ear to the eardrum.

(a) nerve
(b) tunnel
(c) bone

4. When your eardrum vibrates, it makes the _____ in your middle ear move.

(a) endings
(b) nerves
(c) bones

5. Vibrating messages are picked up by _____ in the inner ear.

(a) bones
(b) air
(c) nerve endings

Chapter 8 | Touch, Taste, and Smell

A The Sense of Touch

The largest organ of your body is your **skin.** It covers your whole body. It keeps harmful germs from entering your body. It lets sweat escape. If you get a cut, your body makes new skin.

In your skin are **nerve endings** for the sense of **touch.** Not all these nerve endings react to the same things. Some react to heat and cold. Others react to pain and pressure. Nerve endings for pain tell you that something is wrong with your body. Nerve endings for pressure tell you if an object is heavy or light. They also tell you how rough or smooth an object is. For example, glass feels smooth.

The skin's nerve endings send messages to the brain. The brain then lets you know what your skin is feeling.

Objectives

A1 to name the largest organ of your body

A2 to tell how this organ protects you

A3 to describe what the nerve endings in this organ react to

Check Up

A1 The largest organ of your body is your _____.

A2 This organ keeps harmful _____ from entering your body. This organ makes new _____ if you get a cut.

A3 The nerve endings in this organ react to _____, _____, _____, and _____.

This boy is blind. He is using his sense of touch to tell him the shape of the object he is holding.

Discover for Yourself

Which parts of your body are more sensitive than others?

Materials

- partner
- cork
- flat toothpicks

Procedure

1. Stick the pointed ends of three toothpicks about 1 cm apart into the cork.

2. Have your partner close his or her eyes. Touch the back of your partner's hand lightly with the tooth-picks. Ask if he or she feels one, two, or three toothpicks.

3. Next touch your partner on those parts of the body listed on the chart below. Touch each place three times using a different number of toothpicks each time.

4. Record on the chart how many toothpicks you used each time. Also record how many toothpicks your partner felt each time.

	Time 1		Time 2		Time 3	
	used	felt	used	felt	used	felt
back of hand						
forehead						
fingertips						
leg						
inside of wrist						

Results

1. Was the number of toothpicks you used always the same as the number your partner felt? _____

2. For which part of the body did your partner have the fewest correct guesses? _____

3. For which part of the body did your partner have the most correct guesses? _____

4. Which do you think are the most sensitive parts of the body? _____

Use soap and warm water to wash your face and hands regularly.

B Taking Care of Your Skin

Have you ever scraped your knee? Then you know that it hurts for a while. Soon the skin's nerve endings for pain stop sending messages to the brain. The scraped knee stops hurting. New skin starts to grow over the scrape.

The skin is a protective covering for your body. It keeps harmful germs from getting into your body. When you cut the skin, germs may get into the body. So cuts and scrapes must be taken care of until new skin grows. It is important to wash cuts and scrapes right away with soap and water. Sometimes an **antiseptic** may be used to kill germs that may be in the cut. A bandage may be put over the cut to keep out harmful germs.

Your skin should be washed regularly. Washing removes dirt in which germs are found. Washing keeps the **pores,** or tiny holes, of the skin clean. Then sweat can escape through the skin's pores.

Objectives

B1 to describe how the skin protects your body from germs

B2 to recognize that an antiseptic is sometimes used for cuts

B3 to list why the skin should be washed

B4 to tell what plant can cause a problem with your skin

93

Sometimes other things happen to your skin. Touching the leaves of a poison ivy plant may cause a rash that itches a lot. You can even get it by touching a pet that has brushed against the leaves. It is important to wash your hands right away if you think you have touched poison ivy.

There are some skin diseases you can catch from other people. Usually a doctor has to give you medicine for these diseases. Sometimes you can catch head lice from your classmates. You have to wash your hair with a special medicine to get rid of these tiny insects.

Check Up

B1 Your skin helps to _____ your body from harmful germs.

B2 An antiseptic may be used on a cut to kill

_____.

B3 Washing the skin helps keep the _____ of the skin clean so sweat can leave your body. Washing also removes dirt in which _____ can grow.

B4 Touching _____ can cause a rash that itches a lot.

Learn to recognize poison ivy. If you do touch it, wash your skin right away.

Nerve endings help this family taste their food. Find out where these endings are located.

C Nerve Endings of Your Tongue and Nose

Your **tongue** is the sense organ for **taste**. It has many nerve endings called **taste buds.** Taste buds react to the food you eat. Each piece of food you put in your mouth sends a message to the brain. A dill pickle sends one kind of message to your brain. Orange juice sends another kind of message.

Your **nose** is the sense organ for **smell.** Air enters your nose through **nostrils.** The nostrils are the openings in the front of your nose. Nerve endings for smell line the inside of your nose. They react to odors in the air you breathe, and they send messages to the brain. If you closed your eyes, would you be able to tell what you are smelling? Would you be able to tell soap from pumpkin pie using your sense of smell?

Nerve endings react to light, sound, heat, cold, pain, pressure, taste, and odor. Things that cause nerve endings to react are called **stimuli.**

Objectives

C1 to tell where the nerve endings for taste are found

C2 to explain where the nerve endings for smell are found

C3 to recognize what stimuli are

Check Up

C1 Nerve endings for taste are found in the

_____. They are called _____.

C2 Nerve endings for smell line the inside of

your _____.

C3 Things that cause nerve endings to react are

called _____.

Objective

D to explain why you cannot taste food when you have a cold

Do you remember the last time you had a bad cold and a stuffy nose? You probably could not taste the food you ate. Do you know why?

Far back in your throat behind your tongue, there is an opening. This opening leads to your nose. Some of the odors from the food you eat go into the opening. The odors are stimuli. They cause the nerve endings for smell to react. Your brain gets messages from your taste buds and your nose at the same time. What you think is the taste of food may be its smell.

When you have a cold, the nerve endings for smell are covered with a fluid. They do not react to odors. Since you cannot smell, you cannot taste. So the two senses must work together.

D When you have a cold your nerve endings for smell cannot react to _____. So your food does not have much _____.

We can enjoy the beautiful scent of flowers by using our sense of smell.

Discover for Yourself

Can you fool the sense of taste?

Materials

- partner
- blindfold
- piece of apple, raw potato, dill pickle, and other foods

Procedure

1. Have your partner put on the blindfold.
2. Hold a piece of apple under your partner's nose. At the same time, put a small piece of raw potato in your partner's mouth.
3. Now hold a piece of apple under your partner's nose and put a small piece of dill pickle in your partner's mouth.
4. Continue using other foods.

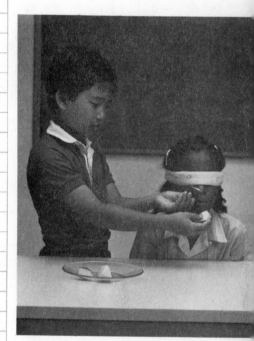

Results

1. What did your partner taste when you put the raw potato in his or her mouth? _____

2. What did your partner taste when you put the piece of dill pickle in his or her mouth? _____

_____

3. Which foods did your partner guess right? _____

_____

4. What kind of foods are hardest to fool your sense of taste? _____

5. How does your nose affect taste? _____

_____

_____

E Taking Care of Your Nose and Mouth

Objectives

E1 to tell what nerve endings are deadened by smoking

E2 to explain how brushing your teeth helps your taste buds to react

E3 to recognize why it is important to be careful about what you put in your nose and mouth

People who smoke cannot smell or taste as well as people who do not smoke. Smoke deadens the nerve endings for smell and taste. People who stop smoking often find that food begins to taste and smell better.

Do you know that food with sugar is not good for your teeth? Sugar helps make cavities, or holes, in your teeth. If you like sweets, try eating fruit instead of candy. Be sure to brush your teeth as often as possible.

Brushing your teeth and flossing between them also makes food taste better. Brushing and flossing remove old bits of food from the spaces between your teeth. If old food stays in your mouth, it deadens your taste buds. Brushing and flossing help make your mouth fresh and clean.

Your teeth are for biting and chewing food. Never use your teeth for other things, like cracking nuts. This could damage your teeth or cause them to break.

Strange objects put in your mouth might harm your mouth or choke you. You also should not put objects into your nose. Such things might harm your nose or make it hard to breathe.

These boys are enjoying a healthy school lunch outdoors.

Check Up

E1 Smoking deadens the nerve endings for

_____ and _____.

E2 You can improve your sense of taste by

_____ and _____ your teeth.

E3 You should use your teeth only for biting and

chewing _____. Strange objects should

never be put in your _____ or _____.

Chapter Summary

- The skin is the largest organ of the body.
- Nerve endings for the sense of touch are in the skin.
- The skin is a protective coating for the body. It should be kept clean.
- Some plants and insects can cause skin problems.
- Taste buds are nerve endings in the tongue.
- Nostrils of the nose are lined with nerve endings for smell.
- Nerve endings react to stimuli. Light, sound, heat, cold, pain, pressure, taste, and odor are all stimuli.
- Taste and smell work together. Smoking and colds deaden nerve endings for taste and smell.
- Proper eating and good brushing and flossing habits are important for the teeth and mouth.
- Strange items put in the nose and mouth can cause harm and make it hard to breathe.

Testing for Allergies

Do your eyelids swell when you pet a dog or cat? Do you get a stuffy nose and itchy eyes in the spring or fall? If you do, you may have an allergy. An allergy is a sensitivity to certain substances that a person has touched, eaten, or breathed. The body "fights back" with a sneeze, a rash, or other sudden signs called reactions. Most allergies just make a person uncomfortable, but a few allergies can make a person very sick.

Certain weeds cause allergies.

100

A doctor can find out which things cause a person to have an allergy. Once that is known, the person can try to stay away from those things. The doctor does an allergy test. This is done by making tiny painless scratches on the skin of the arm or back. Then the doctor touches each little scratch with a small drop of different liquids. Each liquid is from something that can cause an allergy. Animal fur, insect bites, dusts, and certain foods are common things that cause allergies. The doctor labels each scratch to know which liquid was put where.

After 15 minutes the doctor checks the scratches. A red swollen scratch shows that the person has an allergy. Sometimes a person reacts to none of the liquids or just a few. Some people have allergies to many things. The doctor tells the person what the test showed. Then the person will know what to stay away from and what is safe to enjoy.

Problem Solving

One very cold day, Sally played outside too long after school. When she came inside, she stubbed her toe, but she didn't feel any pain. Half an hour later, Sally discovered that her toe had been bleeding.

Why didn't Sally know that her toe started bleeding right after she'd stubbed it? Why is it important for us to feel pain?

Step 1 Make a problem solving plan. Discuss the questions with the class.

Step 2 Gather information. Read about what nerve endings do.

Step 3 Organize your information. List the things that nerve endings respond to.

Step 4 Analyze your information. Tell how your nerve endings would react if you touched different stimuli.

Step 5 Generalize. Do nerve endings protect you?

Step 6 Make a decision. As you have read about nerve endings, you have probably been thinking about whether or not it is important to feel pain. Is it? Why?

In each sentence there is a word missing. Look for the missing word in the list at the side of the page. Then, fill in the blank with the correct word.

pores
fingertips
pressure
stimuli
pain
brush and floss

1. Things taste better if you _____ your teeth.

2. Nerve endings for _____ let you know if something is heavy.

3. Nerve endings for _____ let your brain know when you are hurt.

4. The _____ in your skin let sweat leave your body.

5. Nerve endings react to things called _____.

6. Your _____ are more sensitive to touch than your face.

Circle the letter in front of the word that best completes the sentence.

1. Your skin helps keep harmful _____ from entering your body.

(a) insects
(b) blood
(c) germs

2. Sometimes _____ may be put on a cut or scrape to kill germs.

(a) water
(b) bandages
(c) antiseptic

3. Foods with _____ may cause cavities in your teeth.

(a) sugar
(b) protein
(c) fat

4. People who _____ cannot smell or taste food as well as people who do not.

(a) talk
(b) smoke
(c) eat

Using Key Words to Skim

How many different healthy food groups are there?

Read the following paragraph. How quickly can you find the answer to the question? Raise your hand when you find the answer.

Food is the fuel that makes your body go and grow. What you eat is very important to your health. There are four different healthy food groups. Choosing the right food from each group can help you be a healthy person.

We need to read for different reasons. Sometimes we read for fun. Sometimes we read to find information. We often read to find the answer to a question.

When we read for fun it is not important that we remember what we read. It is important to remember when we read for information. When we read to find the answer to a question, we should learn to **skim.** This means to quickly look through the reading until we find the answer.

To help us skim we should learn how to find the key words in a question.

How many different healthy food groups are there?

What do you suppose the key words are in the question?

These foods are full of vitamins. Can you tell which food group they belong to?

103

The words **food groups** are the key words. Go back to the paragraph and look for the words **food groups.** Notice that the question is answered in the sentence that has those words.

Read the following questions. Then write the key words in the blank spaces.

1. What household chemicals are harmful?

_____

2. What foods build strong teeth and bones?

_____

3. How does exercise help the lungs?

_____

4. In what food group do you find eggs?

_____

5. How does exercise help you sleep?

_____

Cross-country skiing is a fun, wintertime sport that is good exercise, too.

ICE CREAM INGREDIENTS: MILKFAT, NONFAT MILK, CORN SWEETENERS, SUGAR, WHEY, SWEET CREAM BUTTERMILK, MONO AND DIGLYCERIDES, GUAR GUM, LOCUST BEAN GUM, CELLULOSE GUM, POLYSORBATE 80, CARRAGEENAN, VANILLA EXTRACT, AND ARTIFICIAL COLOR.

COATING INGREDIENTS: MILK CHOCOLATE (SUGAR, FRESH WHOLE MILK, CHOCOLATE LIQUOR), COCONUT OIL, PARTIALLY HYDROGENATED PALM KERNEL AND PALM OILS, LECITHIN AND NATURAL FLAVORS.

CRISPED RICE ADDED TO COATING.   MADE IN U.S.A.

PERCENTAGE OF U.S. RDA

PROTEIN	4	IRON	10
VITAMIN A	10	VITAMIN B$_6$	10
VITAMIN C	0	FOLIC ACID	10
THIAMIN	10	PHOSPHORUS	4
RIBOFLAVIN	10	MAGNESIUM	2
NIACIN	10	ZINC	2
CALCIUM	0	COPPER	4

INGREDIENTS: ENRICHED WHEAT FLOUR, STRAWBERRY FILLING (CORN SYRUP, DEXTROSE, STRAWBERRIES, CRACKERMEAL, WHEAT STARCH, PARTIALLY HYDROGENATED SOYBEAN OIL, APPLES, CITRIC ACID, AND ARTIFICIAL COLOR), SUGAR, PARTIALLY HYDROGENATED SOYBEAN OIL, CORN SYRUP, WHEY, DEXTROSE, SALT, BAKING POWDER, CORN, BAKING SODA, GELATIN, ARTIFICIAL COLORING.

VITAMINS AND IRON: VITAMIN B$_3$ (NIACINAMIDE), IRON, VITAMIN A (PALMITATE), VITAMIN B$_6$ (PYRIDOXINE HYDROCHLORIDE), VITAMIN B$_2$ (RIBOFLAVIN), VITAMIN B$_1$ (THIAMIN HYDROCHLORIDE), AND FOLIC ACID.

CARBOHYDRATE INFORMATION

	ONE PASTRY
STARCH AND RELATED CARBOHYDRATES	23 g
SUCROSE AND OTHER SUGARS	15 g
TOTAL CARBOHYDRATES	38 g

IRON	25	25
VITAMIN D	10	25
VITAMIN B$_6$	25	30
FOLIC ACID	25	25
PHOSPHORUS	2	15
MAGNESIUM	2	6
ZINC	25	30
COPPER	4	4

*CONTAINS LESS THAN 2% OF THE U.S. RDA OF THIS NUTRIENT.

INGREDIENTS: CORN, WHEAT AND OAT FLOUR; SUGAR; PARTIALLY HYDROGENATED VEGETABLE OIL (ONE OR MORE OF: COTTONSEED, COCONUT, SOYBEAN AND PALM); SALT; VITAMIN C (SODIUM ASCORBATE AND ASCORBIC ACID); COLOR ADDED; VITAMIN B$_3$ (NIACINAMIDE); ZINC (ZINC OXIDE); IRON; NATURAL ORANGE, LEMON, CHERRY WITH OTHER NATURAL FLAVORINGS; VITAMIN A (PALMITATE; PROTECTED WITH BHT); VITAMIN B$_6$ (PYRIDOXINE HYDROCHLORIDE); VITAMIN B$_2$ (RIBOFLAVIN); VITAMIN B$_1$ (THIAMIN HYDROCHLORIDE); FOLIC ACID; AND VITAMIN D.

The labels on packages of food tell us what is inside the food. What can you tell about the food just by reading the ingredients?

Read the question below. Write the key words. Then read the paragraph to see how quickly you can find the answer. Write the answer in the blank space after the paragraph.

How did junk food get its name?

Key words: _____

Some people eat too much food that contains sugar. Our bodies do not need a lot of sugar. Some sugar is needed for energy. Food with lots of sugar is sometimes called junk food. Junk food gets its name because this food really does not help our bodies stay healthy. Soda, candy, and cake are examples of junk food.

_____

_____

_____

Unit 3 | Staying Healthy

Most of us begin life as healthy babies. The minute we are born, all the parts of our bodies begin to do their jobs. Our lungs start taking in air. Muscles start our arms and legs kicking and moving. Our stomachs tell us when we are hungry. All the parts of our bodies are ready to work for a lifetime—that is, if they are well taken care of.

Of course, when children are small, parents or other adults are in charge of their health. As people grow up, they begin to make their own health choices. Many of these choices will affect how healthy they will be in later years.

Do you know what choices you can make to keep your body healthy? One is choosing the kinds of food your body needs. Another is not using things that harm your body, like tobacco, drugs, and alcohol. Other choices are getting enough exercise and sleep. Keeping your body healthy is something you can do a lot about.

Chapter 9 Eating to Stay Healthy

A Food That Is Good for You

Joe wants his mother to pack a ham sandwich and a banana for his lunch every day. Do you know what mistake Joe is making? You will after you read this lesson.

First, why do you need food at all? What does it do for you? Just as gas makes a car go, food is the fuel that makes you go. Food gives your mind and body the energy you need to do school work, to hit a baseball, or ride a bike. Food gives your body what it needs to make bone, muscle, blood, and skin. Food also helps your body stay well or get better quickly if you are sick or hurt. It is important to eat foods that will do all these things for you.

Your body uses certain parts of different foods for growth and energy. These parts are called **nutrients. Vitamins** and **minerals** are nutrients found in all foods, but there may be a lot of one vitamin or mineral in a certain food, and only a little of another vitamin or mineral. You must eat a variety of foods to make sure you are getting the proper amounts of vitamins and minerals. Now can you explain why Joe is making a mistake to eat the same lunch every day?

The best way to be sure you are eating many kinds of foods each day is to know about the five food groups. There are four healthy food groups. One is the **meat group,** which includes meat, poultry, eggs, fish, nuts, and dried beans. Another is the **milk and dairy group,** which includes milk, yogurt, and cheese. The **fruits and vegetables group** includes carrots, green beans, spinach, broccoli, apples, squash, and other fruits and vegetables. The **breads and cereals group** includes rice, noodles, cereals, and breads.

Objectives

A1 to recognize why you need food

A2 to identify what foods are good for you

A3 to explain how good food helps your body

A healthy meal should contain foods from all four food groups. Which food groups do you see in this picture?

These foods belong to the fruits and vegetables group.

These foods belong to the dairy group.

These foods belong to the breads and cereals group.

Foods in the four healthy food groups help you in different ways. Foods in the meat group give you energy and help build blood, muscle, and skin. You should have at least two servings from this group each day. Foods in the milk and dairy group help build strong teeth and bones. You need at least four servings each day from this group. Foods in the fruits and vegetables group help keep your eyes, skin, and hair healthy. They also help you grow.

Foods in the breads and cereals group keep your nerves healthy and help your body make red blood cells. You should have four servings from the fruits and vegetables group and four from the breads and cereals group each day.

These foods belong to the meat group.

Check Up

A1 People need food to give _____ to their minds and bodies, to build strong bodies, and to keep them _____.

A2 The best way to be sure your body is getting many different kinds of food is to choose food from the four healthy _____ every day.

A3 Good foods help build _____,

_____, _____, _____,

and _____. Foods also give you important _____ and _____.

108

B Foods to Be Careful About

Just as there are foods you do need every day, there are also foods you do not need. Most of the foods you do not need are those in the fifth food group.

The fifth group is called the **fats, sweets, and alcohol group.** Foods in this group are things like butter, margarine, salad dressings, and other fats and oils. Sweets such as sodas, candy, jams and jellies, and syrups are in this group. So are alcohol, wine, and beer.

Foods in the fats, sweets, and alcohol group do little or nothing to help your body grow in healthy ways. They give you very few nutrients. Sometimes they rob your body of needed vitamins and minerals. These unhealthy foods contain too much sugar, salt, and fat.

Some foods also contain chemicals your body does not need. Chocolate and cola drinks, for example, contain caffeine. **Caffeine** is a chemical that can harm your body. Sometimes chemicals are put in foods to make them keep longer or to make them look better. Too much of these chemicals can also be harmful.

Objectives

B1 to identify what foods your body does not need

B2 to explain how these foods harm you

B3 to describe what you can eat instead

These foods contain caffeine.

How can foods that taste so good be harmful? Sugar can make teeth decay. Too much sugar and fat make people gain weight. Being overweight can lead to health problems. Eating too much sugar can even change the way you feel. Some people say they have the "sugar blues," or feelings of sadness, when they eat too much of it. Others get a "sugar buzz," or a jumpy feeling. Filling up on sweet foods and foods with a lot of fat keeps you from eating the foods that help keep your body healthy.

If you work at it, you can train yourself to eat more of the foods that are good for you and less of those that are not. At meals, you can drink low-fat milk instead of whole milk. You can cut fat off of meat and eat the lean parts. When you want a snack, eat fresh fruits and raw vegetables instead of cookies. Low-fat yogurt is a better choice than ice cream. Try whole-grain bread, or cereal, or popcorn without butter in place of doughnuts or cake. Instead of a soda, you could drink fruit juice without sugar or learn to make a shake with low-fat milk and a banana.

Check Up

B1 Many foods your body does not need every day contain too much _____, _____, or _____.

B2 Such foods can make you too full to eat _____ foods.

B3 Some healthy snacks could be raw _____ or fresh _____.

The foods pictured below contain a lot of sugar. Eating too many sweets can cause tooth decay and other health problems.

110

C Things Not to Eat or Use

There are some things that people put in their bodies that are dangerous to their health. Many of these can make a person sick. Some, after long use, can lead to death. There are others that can be harmful even if they are used only once.

Tobacco is harmful, although the effects cannot be seen right away. Smoke harms the lungs when it is breathed in, and serious lung diseases can begin. **Alcohol** is also harmful. Some adults can drink a little alcohol once in a while without problems, but alcohol can make people very sick.

Sometimes people harm their bodies with cleaning products and chemical products found around the house. They may sniff strong glue or try swallowing some cleaning product. This can be very dangerous and can lead to death from poisoning. Many household chemicals can be harmful and should be used with care.

Medicine given to you by a doctor can be very helpful when you are sick. Taking another person's medicine or taking drugs for fun or for other reasons is very foolish. Medicine that is not yours and drugs can cause serious illness, even death. You should take only medicine given to you by your doctor. You should also follow the directions exactly.

Check Up

C _____ and alcohol are harmful to your

body. All household _____ can be harmful.

Medicine that is not yours and _____ can

cause serious illness or death.

Objectives

C to identify what things are harmful to your body

This man is a pharmacist. He carefully measures the medicine that the doctor has ordered.

Discover for Yourself

How can you make a plan for healthy meals?

Materials

- piece of paper
- food chart

Procedure

1. On your paper make a list of how many servings from each food group you need each day.

2. Fill in the chart on the right with foods you like. Be sure there are the right number of servings for each food group.

Results

1. Does your meal plan have the right number of

servings from each food group? _____

2. What foods do you have that contain sugar or fat?

_____

3. For each food listed in your last answer, give a food from the other food groups you could eat or

drink in its place. _____

_____

_____

Breakfast
Lunch
Dinner
Snacks

Chapter Summary

- Food is necessary for the energy needed to do things. Eating food from the four healthy food groups makes your body strong and healthy.
- The meat group of foods that includes meat, poultry, eggs, fish, nuts, and dried beans gives the body energy and helps to build blood, muscle, and skin.
- The milk and dairy group of foods that includes milk, yogurt, and cheese helps to build strong teeth and bones.
- The fruits and vegetables group of foods that includes carrots, green beans, spinach, broccoli, squash, and other fruits and vegetables helps keep your eyes, skin, and hair healthy while helping you grow.
- The breads and cereals group of foods that includes rice, noodles, cereals, and breads helps keep your nerves healthy and helps your body make red blood cells.
- The fats, sweets, and alcohol group of foods have few vitamins and minerals and rob your body of its nutrients.
- Tobacco, alcohol, household chemicals, medicines belonging to others, and drugs can cause serious harm to the body.

Vitamins and Health

These foods all have large amounts of Vitamin C.

Today many people understand that vitamins are needed for good health. They know vitamins help the body live and grow, but 200 years ago people did not know about vitamins. Some people got diseases because they were not eating enough vitamins.

Scurvy is an example of such a disease. It is caused by the lack of vitamin C. People who do not get enough vitamin C have many health problems. Their gums swell and bleed. Cuts on their skin heal slowly. They often catch colds. Their bones can break easily.

A long time ago, sailors often got scurvy. Their diets were poor. They ate dried beef and hard biscuits day after day. In 1753 a Scottish doctor named James Lind made an important discovery. He found that sailors who had scurvy got better when they drank lemon juice. This meant that something in the lemon juice is needed to have healthy skin, bones, and gums. It was later learned there was vitamin C in the lemon juice. The British Navy made sure every sailor got some lemon juice each day.

All vitamins are important for good health. Other diseases can be caused by not getting enough of other vitamins. Eating a balanced diet is the best way to avoid diseases caused by the lack of vitamins.

James Lind discovered that Vitamin C could cure scurvy.

Problem Solving

Eating properly is one of the keys to good health. Are you eating foods from all four healthy food groups each day?

What could you do to improve your diet?

Step 1 Make a problem solving plan. Discuss the problem with your family. Ask them to help you remember all the foods you ate yesterday.

Step 2 Gather information. Make a list of all the foods you ate yesterday. Be sure to include snack foods.

Step 3 Organize your information. Make a chart with headings for each of the five food groups. Write each food from your list under the correct heading. Use a food chart to help you.

Step 4 Analyze your information. Did you eat something from each food group? How many servings did you have from each group? Did you have more fats and sweets than other foods?

Step 5 Generalize. Is your chart typical of the way you eat each day? Is there anything about your eating habits that you would like to change?

Step 6 Make a decision. As you have studied this problem, you have probably thought of ways to improve your diet. What are they?

115

In each sentence there is a word missing. Look for the missing word in the list at the side of the page. Then, fill in the blank with the correct word.

1. Too much _____ can make teeth decay.

2. Tobacco can harm the _____.

3. Eggs belong to the _____ group of foods.

4. Butter and margarine have a lot of _____.

5. Foods in the meat group help build _____, muscle, and skin.

6. Food is the _____ that makes you go.

7. Cola drinks and chocolate contain _____.

fuel
caffeine
blood
sugar
fat
meat
lungs

Circle the letter in front of the word that best completes the sentence.

1. You should have _____ servings from the meat group of foods every day.

(a) one
(b) two
(c) four

2. A snack that is good for you is _____.

(a) cake
(b) buttered popcorn
(c) fresh fruit

3. A food in the milk and dairy group is _____.

(a) cheese
(b) eggs
(c) salad dressing

4. There are _____ healthy food groups.

(a) three
(b) four
(c) five

5. Your body needs only a little bit of _____.

(a) fruit juice
(b) salt
(c) milk

Chapter 10 | Exercising to Stay Healthy

A What Is Exercise?

Do you see people jogging, running, or biking where you live? These are people who know that exercise is important. **Exercise** is something you do to move, stretch, and use your body. Sitting in a chair reading a book is not exercise. Going on a picnic is not exercise. Walking slowly home from school is not exercise.

Objectives

A1 to explain what exercise is

A2 to identify what activities are good exercise

Riding a bicycle is so much fun that it doesn't feel like exercise, but it is.

We all need exercise to stay healthy. A few minutes of exercise will not help your body. Good exercise should go on for a full fifteen to twenty minutes without stopping. Your heart needs to beat fast for that long. Can you see the difference between standing in the swimming pool talking to your friends and swimming across the pool twenty times in a row? Which will do your body the most good? Also, to really help your body, good exercise should be done three times a week.

Good exercises are those in which you move a lot. These can be sports you play with others, such as tennis, soccer, or hockey. Activities you can do by yourself are good, too. Riding a bicycle, swimming, jogging, taking long fast walks, or jumping rope all help your body. These are things you can keep doing by yourself, long after your school years are over.

Check Up

A1 To get good _____, you must move, stretch, and use your _____.

A2 Sports you play with _____ or activities you do _____ can be good exercise.

These people are getting exercise and having fun in a wheelchair race.

118

This girl is preparing to go on a long bike ride.

B How Exercise Helps You

If you get regular exercise, you will be better off than if you do not. First of all, you will feel good. Exercise will help you feel like you have more energy. It will also help you relax and sleep well. It can even help you feel happy about yourself and your life. You will look healthy and feel healthy, too.

When you exercise, you are taking good care of your body. Exercise makes muscles stronger. You breathe deeper, so your heart and lungs work better. Exercise burns fat and helps you keep a good weight. If you exercise, you will have a healthier body. This can help you stay well or recover more quickly if you get sick.

Objectives

B1 to tell how exercise makes you feel

B2 to recognize how exercise helps your body

Check Up

B1 Exercise makes you feel like you have more

_____, helps you _____ at

night, and helps you feel happy about yourself.

B2 Exercise makes your _____ stronger,

and helps your _____ and

_____ work better.

119

Discover for Yourself

Does exercise make your heart beat faster?

Materials

- clock or watch with a second hand

Procedure

1. Sit quietly for at least 10 minutes. Then find your pulse by putting your fingers on your wrist or neck so you can feel the pulse of your heartbeat.
2. Count your pulse beats for 15 seconds. Multiply the number you get by 4. This tells you your pulse rate per minute.
3. Now run in place for 2 minutes.
4. Find your pulse rate again.

Results

1. What was your first pulse rate? _____

2. What was your pulse rate after you ran in place?

_____

3. Was your pulse rate higher or lower the second

time? _____

4. What do you think happens to your heart when

you exercise? _____

_____

C Exercise Safety

Exercise is not dangerous unless you are careless. If you are careless, you can be injured, or hurt. You can cause muscles to cramp, or get tight. You can twist or strain parts of your body. You can fall and get bruises, scrapes, cuts, or broken bones. If you fall on something sharp, you can get a puncture, or hole, in the skin.

There are many things you can do to prevent getting hurt. First, learn the right way to do the exercise you have chosen. Learn from a teacher or from others who can do it well. Remember, it takes time to learn anything new. Each time you begin to exercise, start slowly. Learn **warm-up exercises** that stretch your muscles when you start to exercise. Also learn **cool-down exercises** that help muscles relax at the end of exercise. It is important not to get too tired when you exercise. When you are tired, it is easy to get careless.

Use special care for certain sports. At the pool, do not run and push. Never dive into water unless you know it is deep enough. Never go in the water unless someone else is around. If you bike, skate, or run, do it in safe areas. Stay on a walk where you will not run into things or in a place away from cars. In team sports, do not be rough. Play by the rules and think about your safety and the safety of others.

Objectives

C1 to describe how you can be injured while exercising

C2 to explain how to prevent injuries when you exercise

The above picture shows one way of stretching your muscles to warm up before exercise. Below: An instructor gives safety rules to the swimmers.

Check Up

C1 You can be injured while exercising by being

_____.

C2 You can prevent injuries while exercising if you are careful. Do _____ exercises first and _____ exercises afterward. Always be careful and think about _____.

Chapter Summary

- Exercise is something you do to move, stretch, or use your body.
- Exercise should go on for fifteen to twenty minutes without stopping to do the most good.
- Good exercises are those in which you use your body a lot. They should be done three times a week.
- Exercise will help you feel like you have more energy. You will feel better, sleep better, and be healthier.
- Exercise makes muscles stronger and helps the heart and lungs work better.
- Exercise burns fat and helps you keep a good weight.
- Careless exercise can lead to injuries.
- You should learn to do an exercise the right way. Warm-up and cool-down exercises help prevent injuries.
- Good safety rules should be followed during any exercise.

An Athlete's Best Friend

Bill Tessendorf is the athletic trainer for the Cleveland Browns football team.

Athletes, or those who take part in sports, work hard to do well. Sports trainers work hard to keep athletes fit and strong. People often do not see the sports trainer. The trainer is always helping the athletes behind the scenes. Most high schools, colleges, and professional teams have trainers.

Sports trainers have many important duties. They help athletes get in good shape so they can participate in sports without getting hurt. They help the coach pick out the right equipment to protect different parts of the athletes' bodies. They wrap athletes' knees or wrists to make them stronger.

Sometimes an athlete gets hurt even with this special care. Then the sports trainer gives the athlete first aid. If the athlete has to follow a doctor's order, the trainer helps the athlete take care of the hurt body part. The trainer helps the athlete exercise the part to make it strong again. Trainers know they have done their jobs well when the hurt athlete can take part in the sport again.

Anyone who wants to be a sports trainer must go to college. There he or she will study body sciences, health, medicine, and physical education.

Problem Solving

Many accidents happen on the playground. It is very important to follow safety rules to help avoid these accidents.

Pretend that you are in charge of your school playground. What kinds of safety rules would you have?

Step 1 Make a problem solving plan. Discuss the question with your class.

Step 2 Gather information. Discuss the accidents that have happened or could happen on the different pieces of playground equipment and on the blacktop.

Step 3 Organize your information. List the pieces of equipment and the different playground games. What are the dangers involved in each one?

Step 4 Analyze your information. What can be done to prevent accidents that could happen on the playground?

Step 5 Generalize. Would you say that it is necessary to have safety rules for the playground?

Step 6 Make a decision. As you have been listing the dangers involved in playing on the playground, you have probably thought of many safety rules that you would have if you were in charge of your school playground. What are they?

In each sentence there is a word missing. Look for the missing word in the list at the side of the page. Then, fill in the blank with the correct word.

exercise
fast
feel
muscles
injured
slowly
jumping rope
relax

1. Careless exercise can cause you to be _____.

2. Good exercise helps you to look healthy and _____ healthy.

3. Cool-down exercises help your muscles _____ after exercise.

4. A good exercise to do alone is _____.

5. Your heart and lungs work better when you _____.

6. Always start to exercise _____.

7. Exercise makes your _____ stronger.

8. Your heart needs to beat _____ during exercise.

Circle the letter in front of the word that best completes each sentence.

1. Exercise can be harmful if you _____.

   (a) start fast
   (b) breathe deep
   (c) burn fat

2. A good exercise is _____.

   (a) walking slowly
   (b) reading
   (c) swimming

3. You should get good exercise _____ times a week.

   (a) two
   (b) three
   (c) seven

4. Good exercise should go on for fifteen to twenty _____ without stopping.

   (a) hours
   (b) minutes
   (c) days

Classifying Things

Some things are easier to remember if you classify them. When you classify you make groups. You put things that are alike in the same group.

Look at these words: Mary, Mike, Harvey, Susan, Rosa, Felipe. Are the words alike? Are they different?

A quick look should tell you that all the words are nouns, and all the nouns are names. So the words are alike in two ways. How are they different? Some are girls' names and some are boys' names.

Classify the words by listing them under the group to which they belong.

Look at this list: whale, horse, squirrel, jellyfish, dog, tuna. How would you begin to classify these words.

You can see that each word is a kind of animal. How would you classify the animals? Try classifying them by where they live. They live in one of two places. So they are divided into two groups.

First complete the name of each group. Then list each animal in one of the groups.

Group 1
Girls' Names

_____

_____

_____

Group 2
Boys' Names

_____

_____

_____

Group 1
Animals That
Live on _____

_____

_____

_____

Group 2
Animals That
Live in _____

_____

_____

_____

125

Look at this list of words: truck, racing car, motorboat, canoe, motorcycle, sailboat. Each word is the name of a vehicle, something in which you can travel, but all the objects do not travel on the same thing. There are two groups.

Complete the names of each group. Then classify the vehicles by putting them in one of the groups.

Group A	**Group B**
Travels on _____	**Travels on** _____
_____	_____
_____	_____
_____	_____

Suppose that you have to shop for food. Here is your shopping list.

hamburger	butter	cottage cheese
milk	ham	beef
cream cheese	oranges	potatoes
carrots	chicken	apples

If you follow this shopping list, you will walk back and forth and all over the store to get the food. Make your job easier.

Classify the foods on your list under the sections where they may be found in the store.

Meats	**Produce (fruits and vegetables)**	**Dairy (milk products)**
_____	_____	_____
_____	_____	_____
_____	_____	_____
_____	_____	_____

126

Below is a list of clothing you can wear on certain parts of your body. The clothes can be classified in two groups. First complete the names of the groups. Then classify the clothes.

hat   socks   scarf
shoes   earmuffs   boots
cap   slippers

Things worn on

the _____

_____

_____

_____

Things worn on

the _____

_____

_____

_____

In Unit 1 you learned about the biomes of the earth. One of the biomes you studied is the forest biome. You learned that there are different kinds of forests, and that there are different kinds of plants and animals in the forests.

Below is a list of plants and animals that live in forests. Classify them according to the forest in which they live.

maple tree   hemlock tree   black bear
anteater   monkey   white-tailed-deer
toucan   parrot   redwood tree
bamboo   chipmunk   orchid

**Plants and Animals
of the
North American Forest**

_____

_____

_____

_____

_____

**Plants and Animals
of the
Rain Forest**

_____

_____

_____

_____

_____

Unit 4 | Earth in Space: Land, Air, and Water

Long ago, people thought Earth was flat. They thought if they sailed a ship out over the ocean, they would come to the end of it. They feared they would fall off the edge of Earth.

You can see that early explorers had to be very brave. They did not know what they would find, but they did not fall off the edge. Instead they learned that Earth is round. Once they knew that, they went on to find that there were many more lands and peoples in the world than they had known. They changed people's understanding of the world forever.

What do you suppose those early explorers would have thought if they had been told someday people would go to the moon? You see, we are still exploring unknown parts of our world. We send satellites, rockets, and astronauts into space. We do not know exactly what we will find out about the solar system and the universe beyond. We do not know what new ways we will come to better understand Earth itself.

Chapter 11 Earth in Space

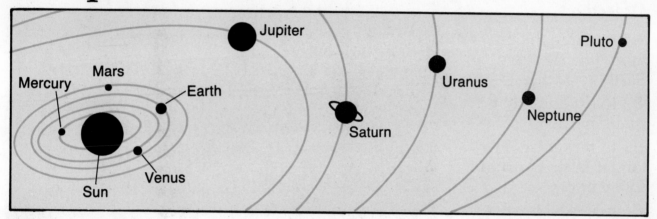

A What Is a Solar System?

Some scientists call our planet, "Spaceship Earth." Earth, however, is not alone on its trip through space. Earth is only one planet in our **solar system.** The sun is the center of the solar system. Circling the sun are nine planets. Some of these planets have one or more moons in **orbit,** a circular path, around them.

Other objects in space are also part of our solar system. Objects with tails called comets circle our sun. Large chunks of rock called meteors also orbit the sun.

Our solar system has nine planets that orbit the sun. Which one is Earth?

Objectives

A1 to identify what the center of our solar system is called

A2 to recognize what Earth is

A3 to name a circular path

A4 to identify what we call space objects with tails

A5 to recognize what a meteor is

Check Up

A1 The _____ is the center of our solar system.

A2 Earth is only one _____ of nine that circle the sun.

A3 This circular path is called an _____.

A4 _____ are space objects with tails. They orbit the sun.

A5 Meteors are large chunks of _____.

129

B How Earth Moves

Objectives

B1 to name the imaginary line through Earth

B2 to explain what rotate means

B3 to recognize how long it takes Earth to rotate once

B4 to describe what revolve means

B5 to tell how long it takes Earth to revolve around the sun

Can you find the North and the South poles on a globe? Imagine a line that runs from the North Pole to the South Pole through the center of Earth. This imaginary line is called Earth's **axis.** Earth **rotates,** or spins, around this axis. It takes one day, or 24 hours, to make one rotation.

Earth also **revolves,** or travels, around the sun. It takes almost a year for this trip. All the other planets also revolve around the sun. The planets closer to the sun than Earth take less than a year for the trip. Those farther away take more than a year. Can you figure out why this is true?

Check Up

B1 An imaginary line between the North and South poles is called Earth's _____.

B2 Earth rotates or _____ on this line.

B3 It takes _____ to rotate once.

B4 Earth travels or _____ around the sun.

B5 This trip takes about a _____.

Point to the equator and axis on this globe.

130

The moon, left, is Earth's natural satellite.

C Earth Satellites

A **satellite** is an object in space that travels around another object in space. Earth has one natural satellite. Do you know what it is called? It is called the moon. The moon revolves around Earth once every 28 days. As it revolves it rotates once. This means that the moon always keeps the same side turned toward Earth. If you want to see the other side of the moon you will have to take a space ship to it.

Objectives

C1 to identify what a satellite is

C2 to name Earth's natural satellite

Check Up

C1 A space object that revolves around another space object is called a _____.

C2 The natural object that circles Earth is the _____.

Other satellites circle Earth. These satellites were made by people. Some of these satellites reflect or bounce radio and television signals to Earth from different places in the world. Others take pictures of clouds. This helps tell about the weather. Still others can help people talk on the phone to people all over the world.

Check Up

C3 Some satellites made by people reflect radio

_____ back to Earth.

This satellite is man-made. It is used to gather information.

Discover for Yourself

Why can we see only one side of the moon?

Materials

- large ball (basketball, playground ball)
- chalk

Procedure

1. Put a big white chalk mark **X** on one side of the ball.

2. Put a big white chalk mark **O** on the other side of the ball.

3. Have one person walk all the way around the room with the ball. Do not turn the ball when making this trip.

4. Have another person walk all the way around the room, slowly turning the ball so the **X** side always faces the center of the room.

Results

1. What did you see when the person did not turn the ball?

_____

_____

2. What did you see when the person turned the ball as he or she walked around the room?

_____

_____

3. Why do you think that we can see only one side of the moon?

_____

_____

Chapter Summary

- Planet Earth is one of nine planets in our solar system.
- The sun is the center of the solar system.
- Large chunks of rock called meteors also orbit the sun.
- Earth rotates on its axis once every 24 hours.
- Earth revolves around the sun once every year.
- Satellites travel around other objects in space.
- The moon is Earth's natural satellite.
- Satellites made by people are used to reflect radio and television signals, help tell about the weather, and help people talk on the telephone to places all over the world.

The First Modern Astronomer

Nicolaus Copernicus was born in Poland in 1473. In those days people believed that Earth was the center of the universe. Each day they saw the sun and stars in different places in the sky. They guessed that the sun and stars moved around Earth. They thought Earth stood still.

Copernicus is pictured here with some of the tools he used to study astronomy.

Copernicus had a different idea. He thought that Earth rotated, or turned, like a top on its axis. Earth's axis is an imaginary line between the North and South poles. Copernicus also thought that Earth revolved, or moved, around the sun. He thought the sun, not Earth, was the center of the solar system.

Today, we know a lot more about the solar system. We have powerful telescopes that let us see into the heavens. We have space flights that bring us information. We have machines that measure motion and distance. We know that Copernicus was right. Earth does spin on its axis to make day and night. Earth does move around the sun to give us our seasons. The sun is the center of our solar system.

Many other discoveries about Earth, the sun, and stars were based on Copernicus' ideas. For this reason, Copernicus is remembered as the first modern astronomer.

Problem Solving

Each planet in our solar system has a different atmosphere, temperature, and surface. All human beings are adapted to life on Earth, but they could not survive on the other planets. Why is this true? What could be done to help humans survive on other planets?

Step 1 Make a problem solving plan. Discuss the questions with the class.

Step 2 Gather information. Read about the conditions on the planet Mars in an encyclopedia or library book.

Step 3 Organize your information. List the conditions on Mars.

Step 4 Analyze your information. How are these conditions different from those on Earth?

Step 5 Generalize. Can a human being survive in these conditions?

Step 6 Make a decision. As you have been reading about conditions on Mars, you have probably been thinking about what conditions would have to be created for humans to survive on that planet. What are they?

In each sentence there is a word missing. Look for the missing word in the list at the side of the page. Then, fill in the blank with the correct word.

1. Earth _____ around the sun.

2. The moon takes about _____ days to circle Earth.

3. _____ are large chunks of space rocks.

4. Earth _____ on its axis.

5. The _____ is a natural Earth satellite.

6. Earth spins on its axis once every _____.

7. Space objects with tails are _____.

8. It takes about one _____ for Earth to revolve around the sun.

9. The _____ is the center of the solar system.

10. There are _____ planets.

day
year
28
rotates
comets
revolves
9
moon
meteors
sun

Match each word in Column A with the phrase that best describes it in Column B. Write the letter of the phrase in the blank space in Column A.

Column A

_____sun

_____comet

_____meteor

_____moon

Column B

a. Earth's natural satellite

b. a large chunk of space rock

c. an object at the center of the solar system

d. a space object with a tail

Chapter 12 | Land

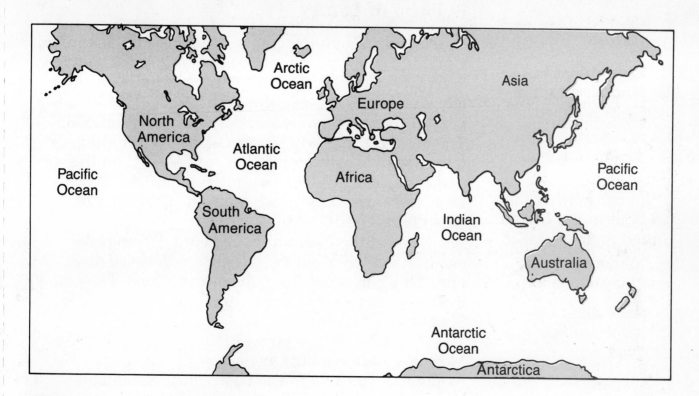

A The Surface of the Earth

Look at the map of the earth. With a blue crayon or pencil, color in the water areas. Use your classroom globe or a colored map to help you. As you can see from your map, most of the earth is covered with water.

The land of the earth is divided into seven large areas. These areas are called **continents.** The continents are named North America, South America, Europe, Asia, Antarctica, Africa, and Australia. Find the seven continents on the map above.

Objectives

A1 to tell what most of the earth's surface is covered with

A2 to name the land areas of the earth

Check Up

A1 Most of the earth's surface is covered with

_____.

A2 The land of the earth is divided into seven areas

called _____.

B Form of Land

Objectives

B1 to tell what the flat land along some seacoasts is called

B2 to describe what old mountains look like

B3 to name what the flat land in the central United States is called

B4 to identify what new mountains look like

Come and take an imaginary trip across the mainland United States. Find out about the land in this country. Start your trip in New York City. As you leave the city, you see that the land is almost flat. This land is a **coastal plain.** Not all seacoasts have a coastal plain. Traveling on, you will see the Appalachian Mountains ahead. These mountains are rounded on the top and covered with trees. Rounded mountains have been worn down by wind and rain. They are **old mountains.**

Beyond the mountains, the land becomes flat again. It stretches out for kilometers in every direction. This flat grassland is the Great Plains. The Great Plains cover much of the central part of the United States.

As you leave the Great Plains, you see the Rocky Mountains ahead. But they are not like the rounded mountains you saw in the East. These mountains have sharp, rocky peaks. Some of their tops are covered with snow. No trees grow on these mountaintops. They are **new mountains.**

As you come near Los Angeles, the land again becomes flat. You end your trip on another coastal plain.

B1 A_____ is flat land near the sea or ocean.

B2 Old mountains have_____ mountaintops.

B3 The flat land in the central United States is known

as the _____.

B4 New mountains have _____, _____

peaks.

These are the Grand Teton mountains, part of the Rocky mountains, in Wyoming. Do you think that they are old or new mountains?

138

C How Mountains Are Formed

There are three main kinds of mountains. They are volcanoes, fault-block mountains, and folded mountains. These mountains are formed in different ways.

Volcanoes are formed when **magma,** or melted rock, seeps or erupts through cracks in the earth's crust. When the melted rock pours from the mountain's crater, it is called **lava.** When lava hardens, it forms a cone-shaped mountain.

Great cracks run through the earth's crust in some places. These cracks are called **faults.** Sometimes pressure within the earth causes the crust to move along a fault. The crust on the side of a fault may move upward. When this happens, a **fault-block mountain** is formed.

Folded mountains are also formed by pressure. On some parts of the earth's crust, there are no faults. So there is no way to get rid of pressure inside the earth. When the pressure inside the earth becomes too great, the crust **folds,** or bends. If the pressure continues, these folds rise higher. When the folds of crust become very high, they form folded mountains.

Check Up

C1 Cone-shaped mountains are formed by _____ coming to the surface of the earth. These mountains are called _____.

C2 Mountains are formed when the crust slips along a crack called a _____. These mountains are called _____ mountains.

C3 When the earth's crust folds over and over, a _____ mountain is formed.

Objectives

C1 to tell how volcanoes are formed

C2 to explain how fault-block mountains are formed

C3 to describe how folded mountains are formed

The mountains in the picture on the left are fault-block mountains. What kind are the mountains on the right?

Discover for Yourself

How are folded and faulted mountains formed?

Materials

- two different colors of modeling clay
- rolling pin
- drawing paper

Procedure

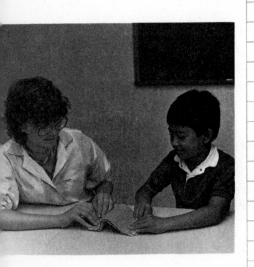

1. Roll out pieces of the modeling clay about 15 cm long, 8 cm wide and ½ cm thick.

2. Place layers of these clay pieces on top of each other. Make the first layer one color, the second a different color. Continue placing different colors on top of one another until there are at least six (6) layers of clay.

3. From each side, push in slowly on the clay.

4. Flatten the clay layers out again and this time hold the ends of the clay pieces tightly in each hand. As quickly as you can, move one hand up and the other down.

Results

1. What happened to the clay layers when they were

pushed in by your hands? _____

_____

2. Draw a picture of the way the clay layers looked when they were pushed in.

3. What happened to the clay layers when you quickly moved the ends up and down with your

hands? _____

_____

4. Draw a picture of the way the clay layers looked when the ends were quickly moved in opposite directions.

Discover for Yourself

How can rain cause soil erosion?

Materials

- lunch tray
- 2 kg of potting soil or sand
- sprinkling can with water

Procedure

1. Empty soil (sand) onto tray, moisten it with a few tablespoons of water, and form different areas of hills and flat places.
2. Tip the sprinkling can over the soil from at least 30 cm above the tray.

Results

1. What happened to the soil landforms when the water was sprinkled on them? _____

_____

2. What happens when a greater amount of water is poured on the soil? _____

_____

3. If grass were growing in this soil, would the erosion be less or greater? _____

4. Why? _____

_____

_____

_____

_____

Chapter Summary

- Most of the earth is covered by water.
- The land of the earth is divided into seven continents.
- A flat coastal plain is present along many seacoasts.
- Old mountains have rounded tops and are covered with trees.
- The flat grassland in the central United States is the Great Plains.
- New mountains have sharp, rocky peaks with no trees. Some may have snow on the peaks.
- Volcanoes are formed when magma erupts. Magma hardens as lava to form cone-shaped mountains.
- Faults are cracks in the earth's crust.
- Fault-block mountains are formed when pressure within the earth causes a fault block to move upward.
- Folded mountains are formed where there are no faults and pressure causes the earth's crust to fold and gradually rise higher.

An Island Is Born

Most of the continents and islands on the earth are very, very old. They are so old that we seem to think they were always here. We forget that land is always being built up or torn down. The island of Surtsey helps us remember that our planet is always changing.

The island of Surtsey was made by a volcano in the ocean near Iceland. In 1963 an underwater volcano erupted. Lava poured into the ocean. The water nearby boiled. Steam shot 6,500 meters into the air. Imagine how surprised the fishermen were!

The volcano kept erupting on and off for the next four years. More and more lava flowed into the ocean. The lava was cooled by the water and got hard. The waves carried some of the lava away, but the hard lava left behind began to form an underwater mountain. The mountain grew tall enough to rise above the surface of the ocean. An island was born. Scientists named this new island after Surtsey, the god of fire.

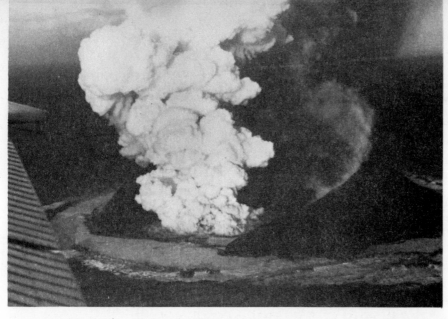

A great underground explosion in 1963 created the island of Surtsey.

Seeds have been carried to Surtsey by birds and the wind. Plants have started to grow in the lava cracks. Scientists are keeping track of each new kind of plant and animal. Surtsey gives scientists a chance to study the early life of a brand-new island.

Problem Solving

Pretend that you live in a deep valley surrounded by steep mountains. You have planted vegetables in the valley, but after every heavy rainfall, more and more of your crops die.

Why are your crops dying? What can you do to keep your crops alive?

Step 1 Make a problem solving plan. Discuss the situation with the class.

Step 2 Gather information. Draw a picture of the crops, the valley, and the mountains during a heavy rainfall.

Step 3 Organize your information. Can you tell what different things happen to the crops as the heavy rains fall on the mountaintops?

Step 4 Analyze your information. How is this rainfall harmful to your crops?

Step 5 Generalize. List other places you could grow crops where heavy rainfall would not be a problem.

Step 6 Make a decision. As you have been thinking about the problems of raising crops in this valley, you have probably decided what you could do to prevent the rainfall from killing your crops. What could you do?

In each sentence there is a word, or words, missing. Look for the missing word(s) in the list at the side of the page. Then, fill in the blank with the correct word(s).

1. Mountains that are rounded and covered with trees are called _____.

2. Melted rock inside the earth is called _____.

3. The large land areas of the earth are called

_____.

4. A _____ is flat land found near an ocean.

5. When melted rock comes to the surface of the earth it is called _____.

6. Cone-shaped mountains formed by lava are called

_____.

7. One look at the sharp peaks of the Rocky Mountains should tell you that they are _____.

8. Great cracks in the earth's surface are called _____.

continents
coastal plain
faults
new mountains
old mountains
lava
volcanoes
magma

Circle the letter in front of the word that best completes the sentence.

1. There are _____ continents in the world.
    (a) five
    (b) seven
    (c) eight

2. The land of the Great Plains is _____.
    (a) hilly
    (b) mountainous
    (c) flat

3. Folded mountains are caused by _____.
    (a) pressure
    (b) earthquakes
    (c) volcanoes

4. Volcanoes are shaped like _____.
    (a) boxes
    (b) cones
    (c) balls

Chapter 13 | Air and Water

You cannot see air in this picture, but you know it is there. Air is puffing out the sail on this sailing board, and moving it across the water.

A What Is Air?

Air surrounds the earth like a huge blanket. This blanket of air is our **atmosphere.** Air, like all other things on earth, is made up of **matter.** Matter may be a **solid** like this book. It may be a **liquid** like water. It may be a **gas** like that used to fill balloons.

Air can contain all three kinds of matter. Solids, like dust blown from the ground, are found in air. Air can also contain the liquid water, which falls as rain. One of the gases found in air is **oxygen.** We need oxygen to breathe.

Objectives

A1 to tell what the blanket of air around the earth is called

A2 to list what the three kinds of matter are

A3 to describe what air contains

A4 to recognize how air can become harmful

Sometimes air can become harmful to living things. When harmful things are put in the air, it is called **air pollution.** Some factories are not careful about what comes out of their chimneys. Cars, trucks, and buses give off harmful gases. Certain weather conditions can prevent air from moving very much. Then harmful things can build up in the air. Air pollution can make it hard to breathe. It can even kill animals and people. Whole forests have been seriously harmed by air pollution.

Check Up

A1 The air that surrounds the earth is called the _____.

A2 Matter may be a _____, a _____, or a _____.

A3 Air may contain solid matter such as _____. It may contain liquid matter such as _____. It contains gases such as _____.

A4 When harmful things are put in the air, it is called _____.

Poisons from factory smokestacks turn the air black or gray. Many large cities have problems with smog. What is smog?

Discover for Yourself

Is air matter?

Materials

- two bottles
- two funnels
- clay
- water

Procedure

1. Label one bottle A and the other, B.
2. Place a funnel in each of the bottles.
3. On bottle B, seal the space between the funnel and neck of the bottle with clay, as shown.
4. Pour water into the funnel in bottle A.
5. Pour water into the funnel in bottle B.

Results

1. Did the water fill up bottle A? _____

2. What happened in bottle B? _____

_____

3. Were the bottles really empty before you poured in the water? _____

4. What was actually in the bottles? _____

5. What happened to the air in bottle A? _____

_____

6. What happened to the air in bottle B? _____

_____

7. Why did this happen? _____

_____

_____

Wind moves these light, fluffy clouds rapidly across the sky.

B How Air Moves

When air is heated it **expands,** or takes up more space. As the air expands it gets lighter. Lighter, warmer air is pushed upward by the cooler, heavier air around it. Air moves when it is heated and cooled. Moving air is called **wind.**

Wind is very important to life on earth. It helps to bring rain to the land. Can you imagine what it would be like if it never rained? Plants and animals would begin to die. Soon there would be little or no life on land. Here is how wind helps.

Some of the water in the ocean changes into a gas called **water vapor.** Water vapor helps to form the **clouds.** The wind blows these clouds over the land. The water vapor changes to liquid and falls as rain. Then the land gets the water it needs for life.

Objectives

B1 to recognize what happens to air when it is heated

B2 to explain what causes wind

B3 to tell how wind is important to life on earth

Check Up

B1 Air _____ when it is heated.

B2 Wind is caused by the _____ and

_____ of air.

B3 Wind brings rain by blowing clouds made up of

_____ over the land.

Discover for Yourself

What happens when you heat air?

Materials

- baby bottle
- balloon
- pot of boiling water

Procedure

1. Put the balloon over the neck of the baby bottle.
2. Let your teacher boil a pot of water for you. Carefully put the bottle in the pot of boiling water.

Results

1. What happened to the balloon? _____

_____

2. Why did this happen? _____

_____

3. Is the air in the balloon lighter or heavier than the

air in the room? _____

C What Is Water Like?

Objectives

C1 to name the color, odor, and taste of water

C2 to identify the three forms of water

C3 to list the temperature at which water freezes, boils, and evaporates

C4 to describe how water can become harmful

You found out that most of the earth is covered with water. Water is different from any other substance on the earth. The difference is due to its **properties.** The properties of a substance tell what a substance is like and how it acts. Here are some properties of water.

Water is clear or colorless. It has no smell. Pure water is odorless. Pure water is also tasteless.

In nature, water is the only substance found as all three forms of matter. As ice it is solid matter. As water vapor in the air, it is a gas. Oceans and rivers are filled with water in liquid form. Another important property of water is the temperature at which it changes its form. Water **freezes,** or changes to ice, at 0° Celsius. It **boils,** or turns to steam, a gas, at 100° Celsius. However, water **evaporates,** or turns to water vapor, at any temperature.

Like air, water can become harmful. When harmful things are put in water, it is called **water pollution.** Some water pollution happens when companies are not careful about waste materials they put in streams or rivers. Sometimes waste materials are stored or pumped underground and get into drinking water supplies. People and other animals who drink the water can become sick or can develop serious diseases.

Check Up

C1 Describe the color, odor, and taste of water.

Water is _____, _____, and

_____.

C2 Water is the only substance found in nature as a

_____, a _____, and a _____.

C3 Water freezes at _____ Celsius and boils

at _____ Celsius. Water changes to

_____ at any temperature.

C4 Water can become harmful when _____

materials are put in streams or rivers.

150

D How Water Moves in Plants

Water is needed for plants to live. If water could not go into the roots and up the stem to the leaves, plants would die. Water can flow upward in a plant. It moves upward against the pull of Earth. Because of this, water can get from the roots to other parts of a plant.

Objective

D to discover how water gets from the roots to other parts of a plant

Check Up

D Water gets from the roots to other parts of the plant by flowing _____.

Discover for Yourself

Can water travel upward?

Materials

- white carnation
- drinking glass
- red ink
- water
- single-edged razor blade

Procedure

1. Carefully cut the stem of the carnation with the razor blade about 15 cm from the flower.
2. Fill the glass with water and a few drops of red ink.
3. Place the cut end of the stem in the colored water. Leave the carnation in the glass for several hours.

Results

1. What happened to the color of the carnation?

_____

2. Why do you think this happened? _____

Chapter Summary

- The atmosphere is the blanket of air around the earth.
- Air is made up of matter that may be a solid, a liquid, a gas, or all three.
- Oxygen, which living things need to breathe, is one of the gases in the air.
- When harmful things are put in the air, it is called air pollution.
- Heated air expands and gets lighter. It is pushed upward by cooler, heavier air, causing wind.
- Wind helps to bring rain by blowing clouds over the land.
- Water vapor from the ocean helps to form clouds, then returns to the earth as rain.
- Pure water is colorless, odorless, and tasteless. These are the properties of water.
- Water can be a solid, a liquid, or a gas.
- When harmful things are put in water, it is called water pollution.
- Water flows upward in plants from the roots to the leaves.

Lake Erie Comes Back to Life

A lake is a lot like a living thing. Lakes can be "alive" with life, and lakes can "die" when there is no life. Lake Erie almost died.

Lake Erie is one of the Great Lakes between the United States and Canada. Many years ago it was a healthy biome. Its water was fresh and clean. Plants and small animals grew and were food for fish. More and more fish were hatched. Fishing in Lake Erie became a big business. The lake was a nice place to enjoy the water.

In time, many people came to live and work near the lake. Factories and houses were built. Garbage and chemicals were thrown into Lake Erie. These poisons killed the fish. Other chemicals went into the lake and made plants grow too fast. The balance of the lake was upset. The lake water became so polluted that people could not drink it. The fish were unsafe for people to eat. Lake Erie was no longer a nice place to visit. It was dirty. It smelled bad.

This photograph shows at least one property of water. Which one?

At almost the last minute, people passed laws to save Lake Erie. It became against the law to dump garbage into the lake. Factories had to find other ways to get rid of chemicals. People used new soaps in their washing machines. The suds from these soaps were safe if they drained into the lake.

These changes started to make Lake Erie's water cleaner. Slowly, the balance between plants and animals came back. Now Lake Erie is a much healthier place for people, plants, and animals.

Problem Solving

We breathe air constantly without really thinking about it. We don't think about the air pressure inside and outside our bodies, either. At sea level, the pressure inside our bodies always equals the pressure outside our bodies.

Skin divers have a problem. Far below the ocean surface, air pressure is much higher than it is on land. When divers are under the water, they need to wear special diving equipment to keep the two air pressures equal. What could happen to a diver who didn't wear the right equipment?

One special condition divers face is called the bends. What is the bends? What should divers do to prevent the bends?

Step 1 Make a problem solving plan. Discuss the questions with the class.

Step 2 Gather information. Read about air pressure and the bends in an encyclopedia or library book.

Step 3 Organize your information. Write a definition of the bends.

Step 4 Analyze your information. Explain how a diver can get the bends. What happens inside the diver's body in this condition?

Step 5 Generalize. Name some other places where you could get the bends because of unequal air pressures.

Step 6 Make a decision. As you have been reading about air pressure and the bends, you have probably thought of ways to prevent the bends, or to cure it if a diver already has it. How can you prevent, or cure the bends?

Test Yourself

In each sentence there is a word, or words, missing. Look for the missing word(s) in the list at the side of the page. Then, fill in the blank with the correct word(s).

1. The _____ of a substance tell you what a substance is like.

2. The heating and cooling of air causes _____.

3. Water freezes at _____ degrees Celsius.

4. Harmful things put in the atmosphere cause

_____.

5. We need the _____ in the air in order to breathe.

6. When air is heated it takes up more _____.

7. Liquid water _____ or turns into a gas at any temperature.

8. Clouds are made up of _____.

oxygen
wind
water vapor
space
properties
evaporates
zero
air pollution

Circle the letter in front of the word that best completes the sentence.

1. The blanket of air around the earth is called

the _____.

(a) sky
(b) universe
(c) atmosphere

2. _____ pollution happens when harmful things are put in rivers and streams.

(a) Water
(b) Air
(c) Wind

3. Pure water has _____.

(a) some color
(b) blue color
(c) no color

4. When water is heated to 100° Celsius it _____.

(a) condenses
(b) boils
(c) melts

Seeing Cause and Effect

Look at the pictures. What happened? _____

_____

Why did it happen? _____

_____

 The two pictures show *cause and effect*. The cause is the cat jumping on the table. The effect is the broken vase of flowers. When you tell the cause, you are answering the question: Why did it happen? When you tell the effect, you are answering the question: What happened?

Look at this park. What happened? _____

_____

Why did it happen? _____

_____

What is the cause? _____

What is the effect? _____

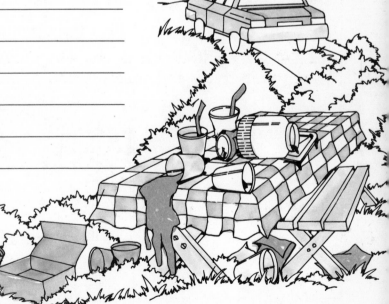

155

Everything that happens has at least one cause. Read the mini stories below. Then draw one line under the cause. Draw two lines under the effect. The first one is done for you.

1. Jody's mother asked her to blow up balloons for the party. Jody blew too much air into the first balloon. The balloon broke.

2. David dressed in a hurry this morning. He forgot to tie his shoes. He took three steps and fell on his nose.

3. When Jane breathed on a hand mirror, she saw the mirror fog up.

4. Mr. Taylor got a ticket because he drove through a red light.

5. Paul failed the math test because he forgot to study.

6. Day and night is caused by the spinning of the earth.

7. Heavy rain was the reason for the flood in the desert.

8. The youngsters were celebrating because it was Chinese New Year.

9. You are able to mark these sentences because you are following directions.

10. I put up my umbrella when it started to rain.

Look at the two sets of pictures. Each set shows a cause and an effect. Under each picture write either cause or effect.

Unit 5 | Magnetism and Electricity

Look at the lights of this city at night. Imagine a night when the lights do not come on. Nothing else that needs electricity can work either. What would happen?

People would have to use candles and flashlights in their homes. Elevators would stop. People who ride subways could not get home. The streets would be dark without street lights. Shops would have to close. Electric stoves could not be used and refrigerators would not keep food cold. No one could even watch television.

What you have just imagined is called a "blackout." Sometimes blackouts really can happen. They happen when too many people use too much electricity at the same time. A blackout could also happen when some machinery making electricity breaks down. Usually a blackout lasts only a few hours. At a moment like that, everyone learns how important electricity is in our lives.

Chapter 14 | Magnets

These children are using magnets to lift paper clips. What do you think the paper clips are made of?

A Magnetic Rock

People first noticed magnets about 2,000 years ago. There are many stories about how magnets were discovered. One story is about a boy named Magnes. Magnes was a shepherd boy who lived long ago in Greece. He used a shepherd's crook made of iron. One day, to his great surprise, the crook stuck to a rock. When people saw this they called the rock **magnetic.** Why do you think they gave the rock that name?

One kind of magnetic rock is called **lodestone.** Lodestone contains a kind of iron called **magnetite.** It is the magnetite that makes lodestone a magnet. Magnets pick up or stick to certain metals. They can pick up steel paper clips. They cannot pick up rubber bands.

The people of ancient China learned how to use lodestone to find direction. They made the first compass using lodestone.

Objectives

A1 to name a kind of magnetic rock

A2 to describe what makes rock magnetic

A3 to tell what kind of objects magnets pick up

Check Up

A1 One kind of magnetic rock is called _____ .

A2 This rock contains a kind of iron called

_____ that makes it a magnet.

A3 Magnets pick up _____ ,

but they do not pick up _____ .

B Kinds of Magnets

Magnets are made in different sizes and shapes. Look at the different shapes shown below. What is each one called?

These magnets usually keep their magnetism for a long time. They are called **permanent magnets.** Most permanent magnets are made of iron or steel.

Pick up one steel paper clip with a permanent magnet. Then try to pick up another steel clip with the first clip. The first clip has become a magnet. So you can pick up the second clip with the first. Take away the permanent magnet. The first clip will hold the second clip only for a short time. The paper clip is a **temporary magnet.** It keeps its magnetism for a short time.

Check Up

B1 Some of the shapes magnets come in are

———————, ———————, ———————,

———————, and ———————.

B2 A magnet that keeps its magnetism for a long time is called a ——————— magnet.

B3 A magnet that keeps its magnetism for a short time is a ——————— magnet.

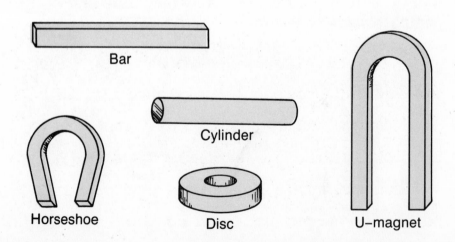

Bar

Cylinder

Horseshoe

Disc

U–magnet

C The Ends of a Magnet

The ends of a magnet are called the **poles.** Look at a bar magnet. Can you see the letters on the poles of the magnet? The letter N stands for north. The letter S stands for south.

Tie a long string around the center of a bar magnet. Then hold it and let it hang free. With a compass find north. Do not hold the compass too close to the magnet. When the magnet stops moving, the north pole of the magnet will be pointing north. The north pole always points north. Just like the earth, a magnet has a north pole and a south pole.

Horseshoe and U-shaped magnets are bar magnets that are bent. The poles of these magnets are closer together than the poles on a bar magnet. Why are horseshoe and U-shaped magnets stronger than bar magnets?

Steel magnets are usually stronger than iron magnets. The strongest magnets include a mixture of **al**uminum, **ni**ckel, and **co**balt. They are called **alnico** magnets.

Objectives

C1 to name the ends of a magnet

C2 to tell what directions the ends of a magnet point toward

C3 to tell what the strongest magnet is made of

Check Up

C1 The ends of a magnet are called the _____.

C2 One end points _____ and the other end

points _____.

C3 An alnico magnet is made of a _____ of

metals. It is the _____ magnet.

Point to the poles on the magnet.

161

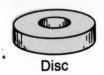

Disc

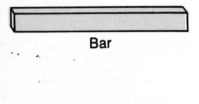

Bar

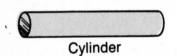

Cylinder

Discover for Yourself

What kinds of objects are attracted by magnets?

Materials

- magnet
- paper clip
- aluminum foil
- iron nail
- pins
- cardboard
- penny
- thumbtack
- hairpin
- plastic button
- pencil
- other similar objects

Procedure

1. One at a time bring the magnet near each object listed on the chart.
2. Put a check mark in the ATTRACTED column if the object sticks to the magnet. Put a check mark in the NOT ATTRACTED column if the object does not stick to the magnet.
3. When finished, group the objects that were attracted by the magnet. Observe them.

Results

1. How are they alike? _____

_____

2. Would you name the group METALS or NON-

METALS? _____

_____

162

OBJECT	ATTRACTED	NOT ATTRACTED
paper clip		
aluminum foil		
iron nail		
pins		
cardboard		
penny		
thumbtack		
hairpin		
plastic button		
pencil		

Horseshoe

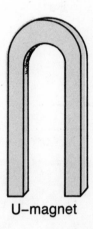

U–magnet

Chapter Summary

- Lodestone is a magnetic rock that contains magnetite.
- Magnets attract certain metals.
- Magnets are made in different sizes and shapes.
- Permanent magnets keep their magnetism for a long time. Temporary magnets do not.
- The ends of magnets are called poles.
- The north pole of a magnet always points north.
- Steel magnets are usually stronger than iron magnets. Alnico magnets, made of a mixture of aluminum, nickel, and cobalt, are even stronger.

A Tool for Discovery

This picture shows a compass that was used in the 1400's.

A magnet led to the discovery of North America! The compass was an important tool for Christopher Columbus and other early explorers. The needle in a compass is a bar magnet which always points north. In this way the compass is useful for finding direction.

Before the compass, sailors stayed close to land to keep from getting lost. For short trips away from land, they used the sun and stars to guide them. But cloudy weather made this dangerous.

It is thought that the first compass was used by the Chinese almost a thousand years ago. The early compass was a piece of magnetic iron placed on a straw or cork floating in a bowl of water. Arab sailors learned of the compass and shared it with sailors from Europe. By 1400 most European sailors were using a compass.

Without a compass Christopher Columbus would not have made his trip to the New World in 1492. His ships sailed for more than a month without seeing land. Because of the compass, he was able to find his way back home.

The success of Columbus led others to explore far from home. This started an age of discovery when much was learned about the world.

Problem Solving

If you were asked to come up with a way to keep an iron nail up in the air without having anything attached to it, how could you do this using magnets?

Step 1 Make a problem solving plan. Discuss the question with the class.

Step 2 Gather information. Read more about different kinds of magnets and ways in which they are used.

Step 3 Organize your information. Make a simple drawing of each kind of magnet. Label each drawing with its name and one way in which it's used. An example is listed below.

	Kind of magnet	Uses
N S	bar magnet	compass

Step 4 Analyze your information. Which of these magnets do you think would work best to hold up a nail? How many would you need?

Step 5 Generalize. Using the magnets think of different ways you could suspend the nail without having anything attached to it.

Step 6 Make a decision. After having thought of ways to arrange or construct the magnets to hold up the nail, which would be the best way? Try it to find out.

In each sentence there is a word missing. Look for the missing word in the list at the side of the page. Then, fill in the blank with the correct word.

1. Something made of _____ would not be attracted to a magnet.

2. A _____ magnet keeps its magnetism for a long time.

3. One kind of magnetic rock is called _____.

4. A _____ is a magnet used to find direction.

5. Magnets will _____ things made of iron.

6. The strongest magnet is an _____ magnet.

7. A magnet that loses its magnetism after a short time is a _____ magnet.

8. Lodestone contains a special kind of iron called

_____.

lodestone
compass
permanent
attract
temporary
alnico
magnetite
plastic

Circle the letter in front of the word that best completes the sentence.

1. Most permanent magnets are made of _____ or steel.

(a) copper
(b) aluminum
(c) iron

2. Magnets are strongest at the _____.

(a) middle
(b) sides
(c) poles

3. A lodestone will pick up or stick to _____.

(a) nonmetals
(b) most metals
(c) plastics

Chapter 15 | Magnetic Forces

A   What Is Magnetic Force?

How can you make something move? You can push it or pull it. A push or a pull is called a **force.** How is magnetic force different from the force you use when you pull a wagon?

Objectives

A1 to identify what a force is

A2 to recognize how strong magnetic force is

Discover for Yourself

Can a magnetic force pull an object without touching it?

Materials

- wooden stand
- U-shaped magnet
- paper clip
- ruler
- scissors
- materials listed on the chart found on page 168

Procedure

1. Slip the magnet into the upper hook (see drawing on this page). Tie string to the lower hook. Cut string to leave about 1 cm between clip and magnet. Tie clip to string.

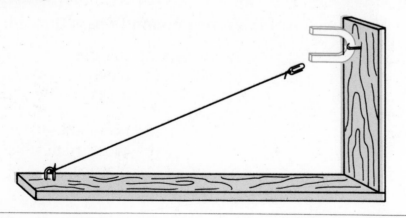

---

2. Pass each material between the clip and the magnet. If the magnet still holds up the clip, put a check mark in the column headed **force passes through.**
3. Take the magnet off the hook. Try to pick up each material listed in the chart with the magnet. If the material is picked up, check the box in the column headed **magnetic.** If it is not picked up, check the box in the **nonmagnetic** column.

Results

MATERIALS	FORCE PASSES THROUGH	MAGNETIC	NONMAGNETIC
paper			
steel scissors			
aluminum foil			
plastic spoon			
metal jar lid			

Check Up

A1 A push or a _____ is a force.

A2 Magnetic force is strong enough to pass through _____ materials.

Discover for Yourself

How do magnets pull and push each other?

Materials

- two bar magnets on which the north (N) and south (S) poles are marked.

Procedure

1. Place magnet A on the desk as shown in Fig. 1. Slowly push magnet B toward magnet A.
2. Place magnet A on the desk as shown in Fig. 2. Slowly push magnet B toward magnet A.
3. Place magnet A on the desk as shown in Fig. 3. Slowly push magnet B toward magnet A.
4. Place magnet A on the desk as shown. Slowly push magnet B toward magnet A, as shown in Fig. 4.

Results

1. What happened to the magnets as shown in Fig. 1?

_____

2. What happened to the magnets as shown in Fig. 2?

_____

3. What happened to the magnets as shown in Fig. 3?

_____

4. What happened to the magnets as shown in Fig. 4?

_____

5. When unlike poles of magnets are brought

together they move _____ each other.

6. When like poles of magnets are brought together

they move _____ each other.

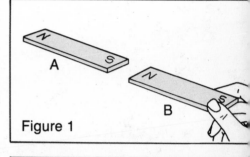

Figure 1

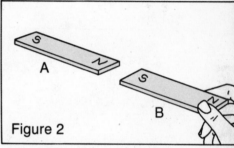

Figure 2

*When poles of magnets pull toward each other, the pull is called **attraction**.*

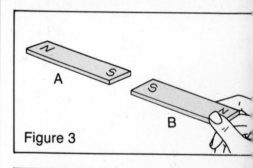

Figure 3

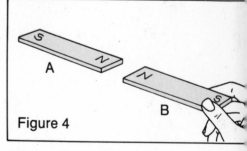

Figure 4

*When poles of magnets push away from each other, the push is called **repulsion**.*

169

Discover for Yourself

How do magnetic forces spread out around a magnet?

Materials

- two bar magnets
- glass plate
- two thin books
- shaker of iron filings
- pencil

Procedure

1. Place the glass on the books as shown in the photo on this page. Put one bar magnet under the glass. Make sure the magnet touches the glass.

2. Hold the shaker of iron filings about 30 cm above the glass. Sprinkle iron filings on the glass. Gently tap the glass several times with a pencil.

Results

1. What do you see? _____

_____

_____

_____

2. Where do most of the iron filings gather? _____

_____

3. Where is the force of the magnet the strongest?

_____

4. Draw a picture of what you see.

170

Procedure

1. Place two bar magnets under the glass as shown in figure A. Sprinkle iron filings on the glass. Tap the glass several times.

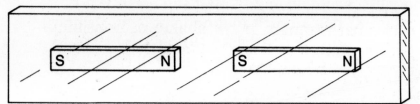

Figure A

Results

1. What is the shape of the magnetic field you see

around the magnets? _____

_____

2. Draw a picture of the magnetic field.

Procedure

1. Place the bar magnets under the glass as shown in figure B. Sprinkle iron filings on the glass. Tap the glass several times.

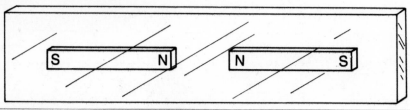

Figure B

Results

1. Draw a picture of the magnetic field you see.

2. What are the lines of force around a magnet called?

_____

3. Where are these lines of force strongest? _____

_____

B Magnets and Compasses

Objective

B to recognize the earth is a huge magnet

Do you know that you are standing on a big, big magnet? Scientists tell us that the earth is a huge magnet. It has a north magnetic pole and a south magnetic pole. A **compass** also has a north and a south pole. This object helps you tell direction.

Discover for Yourself

In which direction does a compass point?

Materials

- compass
- bar magnet with poles marked N and S.

Procedure

1. Carefully bring the N pole of the magnet near the dark side of the pointer of the compass.
2. Next, carefully bring the S pole of the magnet near the dark side of the pointer of the compass.

Results

1. What did you notice when the N pole came close to the dark end of the compass pointer? _____

_____

2. What happened when the S end of the magnet came close to the dark end of the compass pointer?

_____

3. In which direction is the dark end of the needle pointing? _____
4. From what you observed, do you think the earth is a huge magnet? _____

Why? _____

B The earth is like a huge _____. The north-seeking pole of a compass needle points to the earth's _____ pole.

Discover for Yourself

How can you magnetize a needle to make a compass?

Materials
- steel needle
- compass
- dish with some water
- bar magnet
- cork

Procedure
1. Rub a needle about 50 times with the N pole of a bar magnet. Rub in one direction only. Start at the end of the needle and rub toward the point. Then lift the magnet and start at the eye end again.
2. Float the cork in a dish of water. Put your magnetized needle on the cork. Use a real compass to find out which way the point of your needle points.

Results
1. Do the needle and compass line up the same way?

2. Which end of the needle points toward the north?

Procedure
1. Magnetize another needle. This time rub it with the S end of the magnet.
2. Make a compass as before.

Results
1. Which end of this needle points toward the north?

2. Why did you float the cork and needle in the water?

Chapter Summary

- Force is a push or pull.
- A magnetic force is strong enough to pass through nonmagnetic materials.
- Repulsion is the push of magnetic force. Attraction is the pull.
- Like poles of magnets repel and unlike poles attract.
- The forces of a magnet spread out around the magnet forming a magnetic field.
- The earth is a big magnet, with a north magnetic pole and a south magnetic pole.
- A compass has a north and a south pole and helps in telling direction.
- A magnet can be used to separate magnetic materials from nonmagnetic materials.

Putting Magnets to Work

Magnets are fun to play with, but did you know they have many uses? You already know that a compass uses a magnet to help people find direction. Magnets are often put on doors of furniture and refrigerators to hold them closed.

For many things a special magnet called an electromagnet is used. An electromagnet is made when wire is wrapped around a piece of iron. An electric current flows through the wire to make a magnetic force. Electromagnets are stronger than other magnets. They also can be turned on and off.

Huge magnets are used to carry scrap metal.

Doorbells, buzzers, and electric motors all have electromagnets. In factories very large electromagnets lift heavy pieces of metal. They also separate metal from other trash in junkyards. Speakers on radios and televisions use electromagnets to make sounds, and tape recorders use them to record sounds.

A new use for electromagnets is in the "air train" now being tested in Japan and West Germany. This train has no wheels. It "floats" over a metal track. On the bottom of the cars of the train are electromagnets. They pull the train along the track. Such trains make very little noise. They do not add pollution to the air. Air trains have reached speeds of over 500 kilometers per hour.

Problem Solving

Magnetism is helpful to people in many ways. For example, magnets can be useful in finding direction. A compass contains a bar magnet which always points to the magnetic north pole of the earth. This can be helpful to anyone who travels. Hikers, bikers, and airplane pilots are some of the people who use a compass.

There is another kind of instrument that helps people in airports in a much different way. It's called a **magnetometer.** What does this instrument do? How can a magnetometer be used to help airline passengers?

Step 1 Make a problem solving plan. Discuss the question with the class. Has anyone ever seen this machine at the airport?

Step 2 Gather information. Read about the magnetometer in the dictionary, encyclopedia, and other library books. What is a magnetometer?

Step 3 Organize your information. List some different uses for the magnetometer.

Step 4 Analyze your information. What does the magnetometer actually do when a person walks through the machine at an airport?

Step 5 Generalize. What kinds of objects could the magnetometer detect?

Step 6 Make a decision. In what ways can a magnetometer help protect airline passengers?

Test Yourself

In each sentence there is a word missing. Look for the missing word in the list at the side of the page. Then, fill in the blank with the correct word.

1. The south pole of a magnet attracts the _____ pole of another magnet.

2. The lines of force around a magnet are called a magnetic _____.

3. The south pole of a magnet repels the _____ of another magnet.

4. A push or a pull is called a _____.

5. When poles of magnets push away from each other, the push is called _____.

6. The _____ is a huge magnet.

7. Unlike poles of a magnet _____ each other.

force
attract
repulsion
field
earth
north
south

Circle the letter in front of the word that best completes the sentence.

1. Magnetic force passes through _____.

(a) iron
(b) steel
(c) paper

2. If you hold a compass and face east, the needle will point _____.

(a) north
(b) east
(c) northeast

3. A magnet attracts things made of _____.

(a) plastic
(b) cardboard
(c) iron

4. In a magnetic field the lines of force are _____ at the poles.

(a) weakest
(b) strongest
(c) lightest

176

Chapter 16 | Electricity

A power plant is located below the walls of the dam. To make electricity, the water must run down the walls to turn the turbine inside the plant.

A Where Electricity Comes From

A power plant supplies the electricity you use in your home. Where does electricity come from? Much of the electricity used in the United States comes from the power of running water. Power plants are built near the large waterfall of a dam. The falling water turns **turbines,** or large wheels with blades. The turbines turn generators. **Generators** are machines that make electricity.

Some power plants burn coal, oil, or natural gas to heat water. The water is changed into steam. The power of steam is used to turn turbines. A few plants produce power by burning trash.

There are power plants that make heat in another way. They split apart **atoms,** or tiny pieces of matter, to get heat. The heat turns water to steam. These power plants generate a lot of electricity, but there can be problems with waste products and with accidents.

Objectives

A1 to locate where the power to make much of our electricity comes from

A2 to list what fuels are burned to make power in some power plants

Check Up

A1 The power to make much of our electricity comes from falling _____.

A2 Fuels such as _____, _____, and _____ are burned to turn water into steam. Also, atoms are _____ to get heat to turn water into steam.

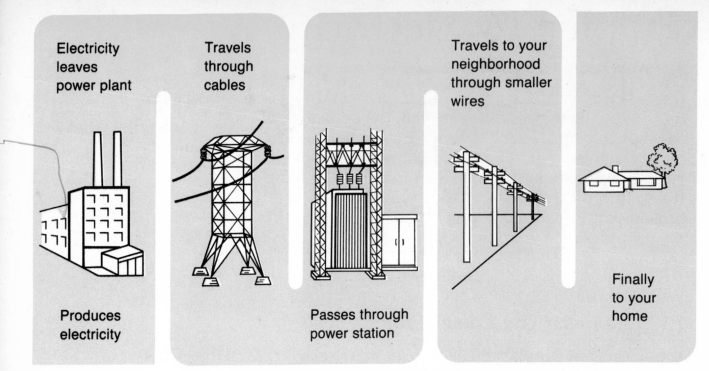

Electricity leaves power plant

Produces electricity

Travels through cables

Passes through power station

Travels to your neighborhood through smaller wires

Finally to your home

Trace the path of electricity from the power plant to your home.

B How Electricity Gets To Your Home

Objective

B to explain how electricity gets from the power plant to your home

You learned that the electricity you use in your home is made at power plants. From there electricity is sent out through very thick wires called **cables.** Tall, strong towers carry these cables. Cables bring electricity to a **power station.** Here it is stored until it is needed. Smaller wires bring electricity from the power station to your home as well as to other places. You may see these smaller wires on the poles along your neighborhood streets. In some cities these wires are located underground.

Check Up

B Electricity leaves the power plant through wires

called _____. Then it goes to a power station

where it is _____. Smaller _____

bring it from the power station to your _____.

C How Electricity Flows

Electricity flows along a path called a **circuit.** If you turn on the light switch on the wall, the bulb on your ceiling lights up. Electricity flows along a wire to the bulb which has a thin wire that glows. It then goes back to the wires in the wall. This is a **closed circuit.** If you turn off the switch, the path is broken. This broken path is called an **open circuit.**

Objective

C to describe what a circuit is

Discover for Yourself

What is a closed circuit? What is an open circuit?

Materials

- 3-volt dry cell
- 3-volt light bulb
- lamp base
- two pieces of bell wire about 30 cm long
- ruler

Procedure

1. Strip about 2.5 cm of covering off the ends of each of the wires. Hook up the dry cell, wires, lamp bulb, and lamp base as shown in the diagram on this page.

2. Now, lift one of the wires from the dry cell.

Results

1. What happened to the bulb when the wires were connected? _____

2. Lift one of the wires from the dry cell. What happened to the lamp? Why? _____

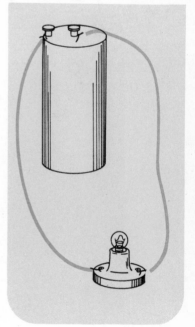

Check Up

C A circuit is a _____ along which electricity flows.

Discover for Yourself

How does a switch turn electricity on and off?

Materials

- 3-volt dry cell
- 3-volt light bulb
- lamp base
- switch

- two pieces of bell wire about 30 cm long
- piece of bell wire about 15 cm long

Procedure

Hook up the dry cell, wires, lamp, lamp base, and switch as shown in the diagram on this page.

Results

1. Is the lamp lighted? _____

2. Is this an open or closed circuit? _____

Procedure

Press the metal down so it touches the nail.

Results

1. Does the lamp light? _____

2. Is this an open or closed circuit? _____

3. How does a switch turn electricity off and on?

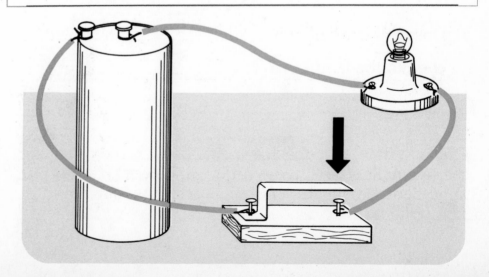

D Conductors and Nonconductors

Some materials let electricity flow through them easily. These materials are called **conductors.** Other materials do not let electricity flow through them easily. They are called **nonconductors.**

Objective

D to list the names of some materials through which electricity flows and doesn't flow

Check Up

D Electricity flows through ―――――――――――,

but not through ――――――――――.

Discover for Yourself

What kinds of things conduct electricity?

Materials

- materials used in the previous activity on page 180
- materials listed on the top of page 182
- piece of wood with a nail at each end

Procedure

Set up the circuit as shown in the diagram on this page.

Results

1. Does the lamp light? ―――――――――――

2. Why? ―――――――――――

Procedure

One at a time, place each material listed below across the two nails so that it lies on the nail heads. If the lamp lights, write yes on the line after the material. If not, write no.

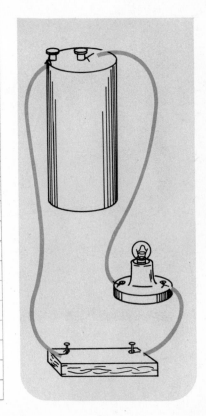

Results

1. Aluminum foil _____   Rubber band _____

Cardboard _____   Steel knife _____

Large paper clip _____   Pencil _____

Iron nail _____   Wood _____   Eraser _____

2. Electric wires are made of metal. Certain materials made the lamp light. What are they made of? _____

_____

3. From what you have seen, what kind of things are good conductors of electricity? _____

_____

4. Electric wires are covered with rubber. Why do you think this is done? _____

_____

E Safety Rules for Electricity

Look around outside for places where electricity is at work. Power lines on poles, power stations, street lights, and lights outside houses all have electricity.

In your home, you may have such things as a washing machine, a clothes dryer, a toaster, a television set, a hair dryer, and power tools. In most rooms there are several outlets in the walls where these machines can be plugged into the supply of electricity.

Objectives

E1 to describe what the dangers of electricity are

E2 to explain how you can avoid those dangers

Electricity makes our lives easier and more pleasant. If a person is not careful, electricity can also be dangerous. A painful jolt of electricity is called an **electrical shock.** An electrical shock can shoot through any part of the body. It can cause a person to fall and be hurt. A very strong electrical shock can even cause death. An electrical shock can happen if you are touching something wet or standing in water when you are around electricity.

Electricity can also start fires. This can happen inside your home when something is wrong with the wires, or when a machine you use is not working right. Fires can be started outside when lightning hits a tree during a thunderstorm. Lightning is a form of electricity.

Here are some rules to help keep you safe around electricity:

1. Never play or climb near power lines. If wires have fallen, stay away from them.

2. Never stand in water a wire has fallen into.

3. Never stand under a tree during a thunderstorm.

4. Never poke anything into an electrical outlet.

5. When you pull a plug from an electrical outlet, hold the plug itself, not the cord.

6. Never touch something electrical with something metal. For example, do not put a fork in a toaster.

7. Do not use anything electrical in or near water.

8. Do not touch worn–out electrical wires or plugs.

Check Up

E1 An _____ can cause injury or even

death. Electricity can also start _____.

E2 You can avoid the dangers of electricity by learn-

ing safety _____.

Above, a safety belt is used by electricians to keep them from falling from high utility poles. A teacher, below, shows the class how electricity travels through the neighborhood.

Chapter Summary

- Many electric power plants use the power of running water to make electricity.
- Many power plants burn coal, oil, or natural gas to make electricity. A few burn trash.
- Some power plants split atoms to make electricity.
- Power plants send electricity to power stations through cables. Smaller wires bring electricity from a power station to your home.
- Electricity flows along a path called a circuit.
- A closed circuit allows electricity to flow over the complete path. If the path is broken, it is called an open circuit.
- A switch is used to open and close a circuit.
- Conductors let electricity flow easily. Nonconductors do not.
- Electricity can be dangerous. It can give you a shock or start fires.
- Safety rules should always be followed when you are around electricity.

This is a nuclear power plant.

Energy from Atoms

The most powerful kind of energy known is nuclear energy. It is nuclear energy that makes the heat and light given off by the sun. Yet this great energy comes from tiny bits of matter called atoms. Scientists have discovered how to make nuclear energy on earth. This energy is being used to produce electricity.

The fuel used in nuclear power plants is uranium. Compared to coal, oil, or natural gas, very little uranium is needed to make electricity, and it does not add pollution to the air.

Nuclear power plants are, however, costly to build. Uranium is in limited supply just as coal, oil, and natural gas are. Also, nuclear energy is harmful to living things. So strict laws must be set for building and running nuclear power plants. Safe ways must be found to store waste from the fuel.

However, many people think that nuclear energy is the best answer to the world's energy shortage. They believe the problems of nuclear energy can be solved. For example, scientists are learning about a way to make nuclear energy using hydrogen as the fuel. Hydrogen is one part of water, so there would be no shortage of fuel. In this new process, there is no nuclear waste.

Problem Solving

On cold, dry winter days, you may have touched something in your home or classroom, and received an electrical shock.

What could you do to reduce the chance of getting these shocks?

Step 1 Make a problem solving plan. Discuss the problem with others. Find out if anyone else in your class has ever received an electrical shock.

Step 2 Gather information. Read about static electricity in your dictionary or encyclopedia.

Step 3 Organize your information. Make a list of materials and objects in your home or classroom that might cause you to get a shock.

Step 4 Analyze your information. Do the materials or objects on your list have anything in common?

Step 5 Generalize. What types of materials or objects cause electrical shocks? What kinds of materials or objects do not?

Step 6 Make a decision. As you have studied this problem, you have probably thought of ways to avoid electrical shocks. What are they?

In each sentence there is a word, or words, missing. Look for the missing word(s) in the list at the side of the page. Then, fill in the blank with the correct word(s).

1. One material that does not conduct electricity is _____.

2. If you are careless around electricity, you can get a _____.

3. A _____ is used to open and close a circuit.

4. The electricity used in your school comes from a _____.

5. Electricity will not flow through _____ circuits.

6. A circuit is a _____ along which electricity flows.

7. Electricity travels easily through materials called _____.

8. When you turn a wall switch on you are making a _____ circuit.

power plant
shock
open
closed
conductors
wood
switch
path

Circle the letter in front of the word that best completes the sentence.

1. Cables are heavy _____ that are used to carry electricity.

(a) pipes
(b) ropes
(c) wires

2. Turbines are turned by the energy of moving _____.

(a) water
(b) air
(c) clouds

3. An example of a good conductor is _____.

(a) plastic
(b) paper
(c) copper

4. An example of a poor conductor is _____.

(a) steel
(b) rubber
(c) copper

Recognizing Fact and Opinion

Read the sentence below. Is it a **fact** or an **opinion?**

There are seven continents on planet Earth.

This sentence is a fact. No matter how many times you count, there will be seven continents on Earth.

Now read this sentence.

It probably will snow sometime this week.

This sentence is not a fact. The word *probably* tells you that it is someone's opinion. It may snow this week, but you cannot be sure of this.
Read the following sentences. Decide if the sentence is a fact or an opinion. Look for clue words.

1. Alma's mother is a doctor so Alma probably will be a doctor, too.
2. Kathy will be eight years old on Saturday.
3. David probably will win the 200-meter dash.
4. The thirty-first is the last day in March.

Is It Fact? Is It Opinion?

Read these twenty sentences. Some are facts and some are opinions. Decide which is fact and which is opinion. In the space after each sentence write **fact** or **opinion.**

1. Heating water causes it to boil. _____

2. It might be colder in February than it was in January. _____

3. Scientists think that the new invention will make life easier for the farmer. _____

4. Some scientists think that dinosaurs died out because the climate changed. _____

5. The desert is a very dry, hot place with little rainfall. _____

6. Electricity is used to run motors and light lamps.

_____

7. Much of the fuel oil in this country is used to make electricity. _____

8. Some animals change color with the seasons. This change protects them from their enemies. _____

9. Some scientists think that Mars is the only planet, other than Earth, that has life. _____

10. Horses feed on grass. _____

11. Using antiseptic on a cut will kill harmful germs.

_____

12. The lights went out when the cable from the power plant broke. _____

13. The tall trees shaded the ground so no plants could grow. _____

14. The stream dried up when the beavers built a dam. _____

15. Brushing your teeth will make food taste better.

_____

16. Camels can walk on sand because their feet are flat. _____

17. Penguins can swim in water. _____

18. The tall tree blew over in the strong wind.

_____

19. Putting pencils or sticks in your ear could damage your eardrum. _____

20. Throwing trash on the ground causes pollution.

_____

Unit 6 | Oceanography

At the time this map was drawn, many people thought monsters lived in the oceans. They had no way to find out if this was really true. Very little was known about the oceans.

Now, however, scientists can go deep into the oceans. They study the mountains and valleys on the ocean floor. They learn how ocean waters move. They watch fish and study plant life. They also hunt for ways the ocean can make our lives better now and in the future.

People have always gotten food from the oceans, but someday, we may farm the oceans. We will find ways to make more fish and plants grow and new ways to use them. We already get salt from oceans. Someday we may get much of our fresh water there, too. Scientists know that such fuels and minerals as oil, tin, copper, and iron are under the ocean. They are studying safe ways to get them out. In some places, the oceans' energy is being used to make electricity. Scientists even dream of building whole cities under the oceans.

Chapter 17 | Oceans and Seas

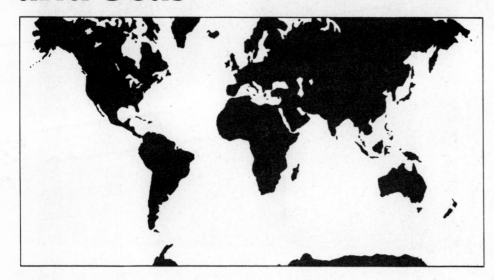

Look at the map. Shaded areas are land. Is the land area or water area bigger?

A Studying Oceans and Seas

Oceans and **seas** are large bodies of salt water. Seas are smaller than oceans. Some seas are surrounded by land. Others are parts of oceans. There are five oceans. The largest is the Pacific Ocean. Next in size is the Atlantic Ocean. The Indian Ocean is about half the size of the Pacific. The Arctic Ocean surrounds the North Pole. The Antarctic Ocean spreads northward from Antarctica.

Oceanography is the study of oceans and seas and everything about them. It deals with living and nonliving things in the waters. It studies how water moves on the ocean's surface. It also studies the bottom of the ocean, or the ocean floor.

Objectives

A1 to find out what oceans and seas are

A2 to list the names of the oceans and where they are found

A3 to find out what oceanography is

Check Up

A1 Oceans and seas are bodies of _____.

A2 Write the names of the oceans in the correct areas on the map above.

A3 Oceanography is the study of _____ and _____.

This ocean-going vessel is used to observe underwater life.

Objectives

B1 to describe what the continental shelf is

B2 to describe what the continental slope is

B The Ocean Floor

Pretend you are on a trip to the ocean floor. Jump into the ocean vessel and take a seat by one of the two windows. The ocean is dark when you are down deep. Turn on the lights so you can see.

Suppose you begin your trip just off the coast of New Jersey. The first thing you will travel over is the **continental shelf.** The continental shelf is a gently sloping plain that stretches out from the edges of most continents. Move to the outer edge of the continental shelf. You will see that the ocean floor drops off very steeply. This is the **continental slope.**

Check Up

B1 The part of the ocean floor that stretches out from most continents is called the _____.

B2 The steep drop at the edge of the shelf is called the _____.

Next you will go over the **continental rise.** It goes on for hundreds of kilometers. On it are many particles of sand, dirt, and shells. Continuing on you will see that the ocean floor becomes very flat. Now you are in deep ocean. This is the **abyssal plain.** The word abyssal means very deep.

Soon you will see mountains. Then you will know you are traveling over the **mid-Atlantic ridge.** You may sight a trench. A **trench** is a long, narrow cut in the ocean floor. It is so deep that you cannot take the vessel to the bottom. The water pressure there is so great that the vessel would be crushed. This trench is one of several in the mid-Atlantic ridge. The ridge goes right down the middle of the Atlantic Ocean.

Keep a lookout for volcanoes. There are many in the ridge. They build up from the ocean floor. Some grow so high that the tops are above the surface of the water. In the Pacific Ocean, the Hawaiian Islands are the tops of volcanoes.

Objectives

B3 to tell where the deep part of the ocean begins

B4 to describe what an ocean trench is

B5 to tell where mountains are found in the Atlantic Ocean

Check Up

B3 Deep ocean begins with an abyssal _____.

B4 An ocean trench is a long, narrow _____ in the ocean _____.

B5 The mountains of the mid-Atlantic ridge go down the _____ of the ocean.

Here is part of the Atlantic Ocean floor.

CONTINENTAL SHELF   CONTINENTAL RISE   ABYSSAL PLAIN   MID–ATLANTIC RIDGE

CONTINENTAL SLOPE

VOLCANO

TRENCH

193

The east coast of Florida is warmed by the sun and the Gulf Stream.

C Currents and Waves

The water in oceans is always moving. One kind of water movement is called a **current.** Currents are like rivers or streams moving through the oceans. Some currents flow near the surface of the ocean. Some flow deep below the surface.

Some currents carry cold water. Some carry warm water. Warm currents travel near the surface of the water. When they are near land, they warm the land as they pass. The Gulf Stream is a current that carries warm water north along the southeastern coast of the United States.

The Gulf Stream begins in the Gulf of Mexico. Wind pushes the current until it reaches the east coast of Florida. From there the Gulf Stream travels north, up the east coast to North Carolina at Hatteras Island. Here the current swings east out into the Atlantic Ocean.

Check Up

C1 Currents are _____ of water moving through the ocean.

C2 The current called the _____ warms the southeastern coast of the United States.

194

Have you ever stood along an ocean and watched the waves crash on the shore? **Waves** are also a kind of water movement. Wind causes most waves to form. Wind is almost always blowing across the oceans. There are no mountains, trees, or buildings. So the force of the wind does not become less and does not change direction. The faster the wind blows, the higher the waves become.

Waves also form as water nears shore. The waves begin to form away from shore. They get larger as they get nearer to the shore. In shallow water near the shore, they break into splashing foam or rolling surf.

Strange as it seems, the water in a wave does not really go anywhere. The waves move across the surface. But water in a wave moves up and down.

Check Up

C3 Most waves are caused by _____.

C4 A wave moves across the _____ of water.

C5 The water in a wave moves _____

and_____.

As the waves get near the shore, they break into splashing foam.

Discover for Yourself

How do ocean currents mix together?

Materials

- large glass fish tank filled half with water.
- pot or container with at least 2 liters of water.
- dark food coloring (red, green, or blue).

Procedure

1. Add a few drops of the food coloring to the 2 liters of water in the pot. Mix it.
2. Hold the pot of colored water over the top of the fish tank.
3. Slowly pour the colored water into the tank.

Results

1. What happened to the water in the fish tank just as the colored water was poured in? _____

_____

2. After a few minutes, how did the water in the tank look? _____

3. Why? _____

Discover for Yourself

What happens when you make waves and currents?

Materials

- fish tank
- water
- cork
- pebbles

Procedure

1. Fill the tank almost to the top with water. Float the cork in the water. Hold a pebble about 30 cm above the water and drop it in the fish tank. Observe what happens.

2. Next blow gently on the surface of the water. Do not blow on the cork. Observe what happens.

3. Now put your finger in the water and move it around and around the edge of the fish tank making a current.

Results

1. Which actions caused waves on the surface of the water?

_____

2. How did the cork move when waves were made?

_____

3. What kind of movement caused the cork to move

around from place to place? _____

_____

4. Which movement of water would carry an empty bottle from Georgia to Hatteras Island? (circle one)

     A. Current   B. Wave

D Tides

Objectives

D1 to explain what causes the water of the oceans to rise and fall

D2 to describe what high tide is

D3 to describe what low tide is

Did you know that the rise and fall of the ocean's water level is caused, in part, by the moon? This rising and falling of the ocean water is called a **tide.** The moon is Earth's nearest neighbor in space. Earth pulls on the moon. The moon pulls on Earth. The pull of the moon makes the water in our oceans bulge, or swell outward. As Earth spins, this bulge moves across the ocean.

When the bulge of water reaches the shore, the water rises up on the shore. This is called **high tide.** As the bulge moves on across the ocean, the water pulls back from the shore. This is called **low tide.** There are two high tides and two low tides each day.

Check Up

D1 The _____, in part, causes the rise and

fall of the ocean's water level. It makes the ocean

water _____.

D2 When the _____ of water rises on shore,

it is _____ tide.

D3 When the _____ of water pulls back

from the shore, it is _____ tide.

If you could stand in space and look at Earth at high tide, it might look like this.

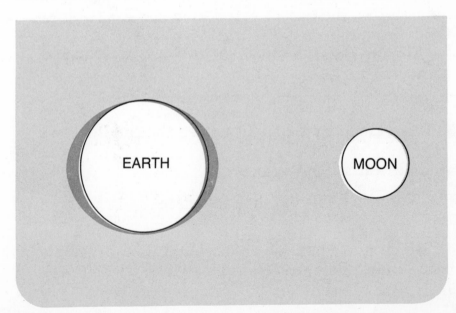

EARTH

MOON

The line across the bottom half of this photograph shows where the water level would be at high tide. Now, the water is at low tide.

When you think of the seashore do you think of sandy beaches? Many shores in the world are sandy. Many others are rocky. There are also many shores that are made up of mud and dirt. These muddy shores are called **wetlands.**

Wetlands are very important to the living things in the ocean. Tiny fish live in the waters of the wetlands. Here they are safe from the larger fish of the ocean. Crabs crawl around on the muddy bottom. Clams live in the mud. Very tiny animals live in the wetlands. These tiny animals are food for the clams and small fish that live there. Wetlands are the beginning of the food chain of the ocean.

At high tide ocean water floods the wetlands. At low tide much of the water falls back into the ocean. Then the water carries some of the tiny wetland animals into the ocean. There they become food for the bigger animals of the oceans.

The wetlands are never dry. There is always some water even at low tide.

Objectives

D4 to name the muddy lands near the ocean

D5 to list the names of three animals that live in these lands

D6 to explain how some animals are moved from wetlands to the ocean

Check Up

D4 The muddy lands near the ocean are called

_____.

D5 Three animals that live there are _____,

_____, and _____.

D6 Tiny animals born in the wetlands are carried to

the ocean at _____ tide.

Chapter Summary

- Oceans and seas are large bodies of salt water. There are five oceans.
- Oceanography is the study of everything about the oceans and seas.
- The ocean floor is made up of the continental shelf, the continental slope, the continental rise, the abyssal plain, ridges, and trenches.
- Ocean currents move through the ocean like rivers or streams. Some are hot, and some are cold.
- Wind causes most waves to form.
- Waves move across the water surface, but the water in a wave moves up and down.
- Tides on Earth are caused, in part, by the moon. Water rises up on the shore at high tide and pulls back from the shore at low tide.
- Wetlands near ocean shores are where the food chain of the ocean begins.

A Wall of Water

A tidal bore is one of nature's most exciting wonders. Imagine a wall of water nearly 8 meters high! Think of that tall wall of water rushing from the ocean into a bay! Now you can understand why people travel from far away to see a tidal bore.

There are tidal bores in many places around the world. These places are very special. They must have three things for a tidal bore to form. First, the bay must get narrower where it meets the ocean. Second, the bay must not be very deep. Third, the ocean's tides must grow very high where the ocean and the low bay come together. Without these three things, the tide comes in its usual slow way.

At high-tide time in these special places a tidal bore happens. The tide rolls toward the narrow, shallow bay. A wall of water builds up. It goes faster and faster. It gets higher and higher. The wide tidal bore goes into the narrow bay with great power. The power makes the water in the rivers that feed the bay flow backward! In Alaska, eagles follow the tidal bore to catch fish. The fish are tossed out of the water by the power of the tidal bore!

These rocks in the Bay of Fundy are called flowerpots. Where do you think they get their name?

After a while the tidal bore gets smaller as it moves up the river. There is a lot of power when it first forms, scientists think this great energy might someday be used to make electricity.

Problem Solving

In every large body of water on earth there are at least two high tides and two low tides every day. We know that the moon is partially responsible for these tides. Why are tides important to life on earth? What would life be like without daily tides?

Step 1 Make a problem solving plan. Discuss the problem with the class.

Step 2 Gather information. Read about tides and wetlands in an encyclopedia or library book.

Step 3 Organize your information. Tell how tides affect life in oceans and seas, and on land.

Step 4 Analyze your information. How do tides affect humans?

Step 5 Generalize. Why are tides important to us?

Step 6 Make a decision. Based on what you have learned about tides and their effect on land and sea, try to imagine life without them. What would it be like?

Test Yourself

In each sentence there is a word, or words, missing. Look for the missing word(s) in the list at the side of the page. Then, fill in the blank with the correct word(s).

1. The _____ stretches out from the edge of most continents.

2. The flat part of the ocean floor is the _____ _____.

3. Some islands are really the tops of _____.

4. Deep in the ocean the water _____ is very great.

5. Waves are mostly caused by the _____.

6. The pull of the moon on Earth causes _____.

7. A deep cut in the ocean floor is called a _____.

8. The study of the oceans and seas of the world is called _____.

9. The muddy lands along the oceans are called _____.

oceanography
volcanoes
tides
continental shelf
wetlands
wind
trench
abyssal plain
pressure

Circle the letter in front of the word that best completes the sentence.

1. The water of the oceans and seas is _____ water.

   (a) salt
   (b) fresh
   (c) current

2. The _____ of the moon makes the water of the oceans bulge.

   (a) size
   (b) shape
   (c) pull

3. The up and down movement of water is called a _____.

   (a) current
   (b) wave
   (c) tide

Chapter 18 | Ocean Plants and Animals

A Seaweeds

All green plants need sunlight in order to live. This is true of ocean plants as well as land plants. Sunlight reaches most places on the land's surface, but it does not reach the deep parts of the oceans.

Masses of algae called **seaweed** grow in the oceans. They need sunlight even though they are not all green. So they do not grow in deep water. There are many kinds of seaweed. Some do not even look like plants. Others look somewhat like land plants, but they do not have roots like land plants. Instead they anchor, or hold, themselves to the ocean floor. They do this with a part called a **holdfast.** Seaweeds do not need roots. Water enters the plant through parts called **fronds.** These parts are like the leaves in land plants.

This seaweed is called green algae. It grows in water that is not very deep. Why do you think this is so?

Objectives

A1 to explain why green plants cannot live in the deep ocean

A2 to recognize why some green ocean plants do not need roots

A3 to identify the name of the leaflike part of some of these plants

Check Up

A1 Green plants need _____ to stay alive.

_____ does not reach deep water.

A2 Many seaweeds have a _____ that anchors them to the ocean floor.

A3 Some seaweeds have leaflike parts called_____.

B The Largest of the Seaweeds

Objectives

B1 to name the largest and fastest growing ocean plant

B2 to explain why some seaweeds have baglike parts

Kelp is the name given to certain kinds of brown seaweed. One place kelp is found is in the Pacific Ocean off the coast of North America. It is the largest and fastest growing plant in the ocean. In fact, some kinds of kelp grow more than 200 centimeters a day! Giant kelp grow to be 65 meters long.

Kelp is found attached to rocks in coastal waters. The holdfasts on kelp are very strong. They keep the plant from being torn loose by waves at high tide. At low tide, the kelp may be found high and dry on the coastal rocks.

Like many seaweeds, some kinds of kelp grow bladders. **Bladders** are small baglike parts that act as floats. The bladders lift the plant upright in the water. This lets the plant get more sunlight. The air bladders of kelp can be the size of golf balls. Undersea divers say that kelp beds look like underwater forests.

Kelp is a very useful plant. It is used in many products. In some parts of the world, it is used as food.

Check Up

B1 The largest and fastest growing ocean plant is

_____. It may grow more than _____

centimeters a day.

B2 Some of these plants have baglike parts called

_____. These special parts lift the plants

upright so that they can get more _____.

Here is a picture of giant kelp. Can you find any of the holdfasts?

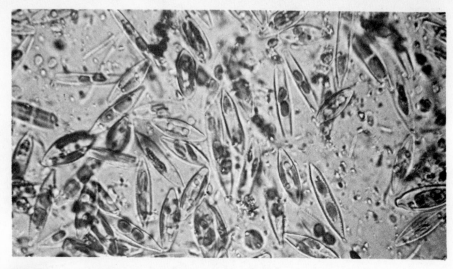

This is a view of plankton through a microscope. These plankton are in one drop of salt water.

C Plankton

Would you be surprised to find out that there are ocean plants and animals so tiny you cannot see them with just your eye? You have to use a microscope. These tiny water plants and animals are called **plankton.**

Plant plankton do not have to anchor themselves. They float near the surface of the ocean. There they get the sunlight they need to make food. **Animal plankton** are not able to move great distances by themselves. They, too, float near the surface of the ocean. They are carried where the ocean currents take them. Plankton are the main food for the small animals of the ocean. They also are the main food for the largest sea animals—the whales.

Plankton are found in all oceans. Both plant and animal plankton float near the ocean surface in very large masses.

Objectives

C1 to identify what plankton are

C2 to explain how plankton move about

C3 to recognize why plankton are important

Check Up

C1 Plankton are groups of very tiny water

_____ and _____.

C2 Plant and animal plankton move with the

_____.

C3 Plankton are the main _____ for small

ocean _____ and for _____.

D Fish

Fish are well-suited for life in the ocean. Study the drawing as you read. The letters point to some parts of the fish.

Most fish swim by moving their bodies. Some **fins** (A) keep a fish from rolling over as it moves through the water. Other fins (B) help a fish change direction as it swims. They also help a fish to stop in the water.

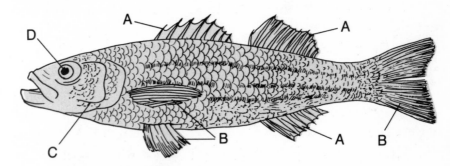

Fish need oxygen in order to live. Fish get this oxygen from air that is in water. Water flows into their open mouths and out through their **gills** (C). As the water flows out, the gills take oxygen from the water.

The eyes (D) of most fish are found on the sides of the head. In this way the fish can see in many directions. Most fish have slimy skins. **Slime** is a sticky material. Most fish have **scales**, or bonelike parts, covering their bodies. The slimy skin and scales keep water from entering the body of the fish.

Check Up

D1 Most fish swim by moving their _____.

D2 Fins help fish to keep from _____, to _____, and to _____.

D3 As water flows out through a fish's _____, oxygen is _____ from the water.

D4 The slimy skin and scales of a fish keep _____ from entering its body.

There are more than 20,000 different kinds of fish. Most live in the ocean. Fish come in many sizes, shapes, and colors. The largest fish is the whale shark. This giant is a very peaceful fish. It feeds on plankton by straining them out of the water as it swims with its mouth open.

Many kinds of fish travel in groups called **schools.** Tuna swim in schools. Some scientists think that fish travel in schools for protection. A large school moving through water may scare away enemies. Others think a large school of fish may attract, or draw, enemies.

Most fish are meat-eaters. This means that they feed on other fish or other animals of the ocean. The strongest and most dangerous fish is the shark. The shark will attack any animal that lives in the ocean. The only enemies of the shark are people.

Check Up

D5 The largest fish in the world is the _____.

D6 Fish, such as the tuna, travel in groups called _____.

D7 The strongest and most dangerous fish is the _____.

It is easy for the shark to move quickly and gracefully through the sea.

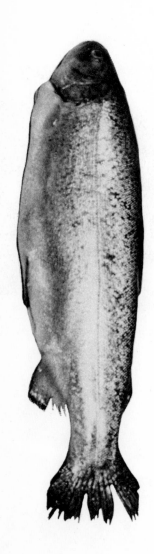

Discover for Yourself

How do fish breathe underwater?

Materials

- whole dead fish from a market
- fine scissors

Procedure

1. Lay the fish flat on the table and look for the slit that runs diagonally behind the eye and mouth.
2. Lift up the flap of skin and look at the structure underneath. These are the gills of the fish.
3. Use the fine scissors and cut away the covering so you can see the gills better.
4. Look in the mouth of the fish.

Results

1. How does the water get to the gills of the fish?

_____

_____

2. You know that there is dissolved oxygen in the water that enters the mouth of the fish. What do you

think happens as the water runs past the gills? _____

_____

_____

Discover for Yourself

What keeps the sea from freezing?

Materials

- three margarine tubs
- water
- salt
- teaspoon
- measuring cup

Procedure

1. In one container mix 120 mL of water and 1 teaspoon of salt. Stir until the salt is completely dissolved. Label this container "Salty 1."

2. In the second container mix 2 teaspoons of salt and 120 mL of water. Stir until salt is dissolved. Label this container "Salty 2."

3. Put 120 mL of plain water in the third container and label it "No Salt."

4. Put all three containers in the freezer. Note the time. Check on the water every half hour until all the containers are frozen.

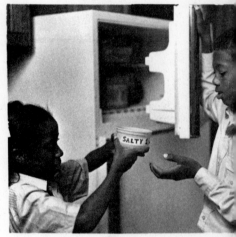

Results

1. What time did you put the containers in the

freezer? _____

2. Which solution froze first? _____

At what time did it freeze? _____

3. Which solution froze second? _____

At what time did it freeze? _____

4. Which solution was frozen last? _____

At what time did it freeze? _____

5. What do the results of your experiment tell you

about salty water? _____

E Mollusks and Other Ocean Animals

Objectives

E1 to explain how clams are protected

E2 to name what clams feed on

E3 to tell what the arms of an octopus are called

E4 to describe how the octopus eats

Did you know that clams and octopuses are related? They both belong to a group known as **mollusks.** Even though they are related, their looks and ways of living are very different.

Most clams live in the muddy or sandy ocean floor near the shore. They are protected by two hard shells that are hinged together, or attached on one side. Clams move and dig into the sand by using a footlike part. They feed by straining plankton out of the water.

The octopus, like the clam, moves by digging into the sand. It moves along the ocean floor on eight long arms called **tentacles.** Each tentacle has many **suction discs.** The discs are flat and round. It uses these discs to catch and hold its food. Crabs and lobsters, which are shellfish, are food for the octopus. The octopus brings the shellfish to its mouth with its tentacles. It cracks the shellfish with its jaws which are like a beak.

Check Up

E1 Clams are protected by their _____.

E2 The food of clams is _____.

E3 The eight arms of the octopus are called

_____.

E4 The octopus uses its _____ to crack the shells of animals it feeds on.

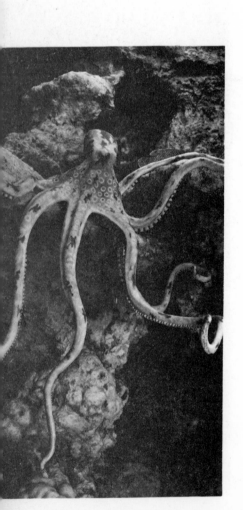

You can see clearly the suction discs on the tentacles of this octopus.

The starfish on the left has six legs, but most starfish have only five. How do you think the starfish got its name? The tentacles of the jellyfish are long and thin. Inside the tentacles are stingers. The stingers are used to get food and to protect the jellyfish.

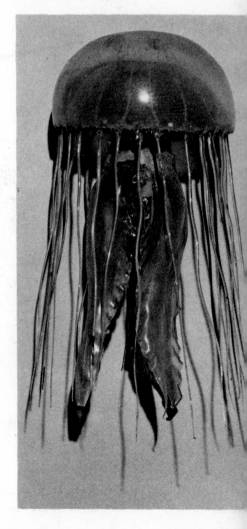

The starfish is not a true fish. Most starfish have five arms, but some have more. Each arm has many little tubelike feet. The starfish moves slowly across the ocean floor on these feet. Starfish feed on clams. They use their feet to pull open the clam's shell. Then an amazing thing happens. The stomach of the starfish goes between the shells into the clam. The stomach takes in the clam. Then the starfish pulls in its stomach and moves on.

Like the starfish, the jellyfish is not a true fish. Jellyfish float with the tides and currents. The main body of a jellyfish looks like a blob of clear jelly. It has an umbrella shape. Hanging down from under the body are tentacles. The jellyfish uses its tentacles to catch small fish for food. When a fish brushes against them, the jellyfish curls its tentacles around the fish. It brings the fish up into its mouth and, then, into its stomach.

Check Up

E5 Starfish move about on tiny _____.

E6 A starfish feeds on clams by putting its

_____ between the shells of the clam.

E7 A jellyfish takes in food with its _____.

It then brings the food up into its _____

and, then, into its _____.

Objectives

F1 to tell what corals are

F2 to describe how coral "rock" forms

F3 to identify what an atoll is

F Corals: the Island Builders

Look at a map of the world. Find the island of Bermuda. It is in the Atlantic Ocean near Florida. Bermuda was built by tiny sea animals no larger than the head of a pin. The animals are known as **corals.**

Corals are related to jellyfish. Like jellyfish they have stinging tentacles. The body of a coral looks like jelly, but corals do not float with ocean currents. They anchor themselves in one place.

The body of the coral makes matter that forms a kind of rock, also called coral. This rock is its home. A coral stretches its tentacles through the opening in its rock home. In this way it catches and eats plankton.

Millions and millions of corals live together. When they die, their rock homes remain. Other corals build on top of these. Very slowly, the coral piles up. In time it may form an island. A coral island is called an **atoll.**

Check Up

F1 Corals are tiny sea _____ no larger

than _____.

F2 Corals produce matter that forms a kind of

_____. Millions of corals live together.

When they die they leave behind their _____

homes.

F3 Slowly the coral piles up to form an _____

called an atoll.

This coral shell is the home of many coral animals.

Discover for Yourself

How does a submarine work?

Materials

- medicine dropper
- straight-sided water glass
- balloon
- rubber band
- water

Procedure

1. Fill the glass with water nearly to the top.
2. Now fill the medicine dropper with water until it just floats in the water.
3. Cut the balloon and stretch it across the top of the glass, securing it with the rubber band.
4. Now push on the balloon and hold for a few seconds.

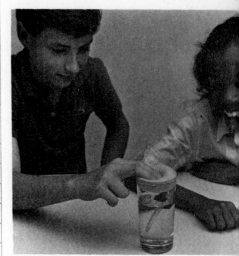

Results

1. What happened when you pushed on the balloon?

_____

2. What happened to the dropper that allowed it to

sink? _____

_____

3. How does it act like a submarine? _____

_____

_____

_____

_____

Chapter Summary

- Green plants cannot live in the deep ocean because sunlight cannot reach them. Seaweeds grow where the water is not so deep.
- Some seaweeds have no roots. They anchor themselves to the ocean floor by holdfasts. They get water through fronds.
- Kelp is the largest seaweed. It grows attached to rocks in coastal waters.
- Plankton are tiny plants and animals that float near the surface of the ocean.
- Plankton are the main food for the small animals of the ocean. They also are the main food for most whales.
- There are more than 20,000 kinds of fish. Most of them live in the ocean. Many travel in schools.
- Fins help a fish swim. Gills help fish get oxygen from the water.
- Clams and octopuses are both kinds of mollusks.
- Corals form a kind of rock that can build up into an atoll.

Farming the Ocean

Everybody knows about farmers who farm the land. Do you know about farmers who farm the ocean?

People who live near the ocean have always taken a lot of their food from the water, but some people have exciting ideas. They make food grow in the ocean just as other farmers do on land. These ocean farmers "plant" oysters in the shallow coast waters. They grow special seaweed to harvest and eat. They raise many small ocean animals in the waters off their coasts.

Other people are trying to make new food out of animals already living in the ocean. One type of these animals is krill. Krill are a very tiny kind of shrimp. They are a good source of protein for many other ocean animals.

Scientists are trying to find ways to use krill as food for land animals and people. What will happen

This ocean farmer is "planting" mussels on poles.

if we take the krill out of the ocean? What will happen to the other ocean animals that eat krill? These are important questions to think about. We have to think about the balance of nature when we start using a natural resource.

Problem Solving

Krill are small, shrimplike creatures that live in the oceans. They are a major food source for the animals of the oceans. People are becoming more and more interested in using krill as food for humans. What do you think are the advantages and disadvantages of taking krill from the oceans to feed humans? Why?

Step 1 Make a problem solving plan. Discuss the question with the class.

Step 2 Gather information. Read about krill in an encyclopedia or library book.

Step 3 Organize your information. Tell how krill are used in the oceans.

Step 4 Analyze your information. How are krill important to the food chain in the ocean?

Step 5 Generalize. How can krill benefit humans?

Step 6 Make a decision. Based on what you have learned about the importance of krill, tell what would happen to the food chains on earth and in the oceans if krill were used as a food source for humans.

In each sentence there is a word, or words, missing. Look for the missing word(s) in the list at the side of the page. Then, fill in the blank with the correct word(s).

1. The shark has only one enemy, _____.

2. All green plants need _____ in order to live and grow.

3. The octopus moves along the ocean floor on long

arms called _____.

4. The largest fish in the sea is the _____.

5. A kind of plant that grows in the ocean is

_____.

6. One sea animal that moves by using a footlike part

is the _____.

7. Some islands are made up of the rocklike parts

made by _____.

8. The _____ is a sea animal that feeds by putting its stomach between the shells of a clam.

sunlight
corals
people
whale shark
starfish
clam
tentacles
seaweed

Circle the letter in front of the word that best completes the sentence.

1. Seaweed cannot grow deep in the ocean because there is no _____.

    (a) soil
    (b) water
    (c) sunlight

2. Whales are large but some feed on tiny plants and animals called _____.

    (a) kelp
    (b) plankton
    (c) bladder

3. A fish can see in almost every direction because its eyes are on the _____ of its head.

    (a) sides
    (b) top
    (c) front

4. The clam and octopus both belong to a group called _____.

    (a) mollusks
    (b) fish
    (c) coral

Chapter 19 | Ocean Ecology

The sea urchin has long, sharp spines that are used for protection. Sometimes the spines are used to dig into rock for shelter.

A Upsetting the Balance of Nature

Living things have a relationship with their environment, or surroundings. They also have a relationship with other living things in that environment. As long as a balance is kept in these relationships, plants and animals can survive. **Ecology** is the study of these relationships and their balance. What does it mean to upset the balance of nature? Let's find out by studying kelp.

About 25 years ago the kelp that grows off the shores of California began to disappear. No one knew what had happened. Then a scientist noticed that the ocean floor where kelp grows was covered with sea urchins. These spiny sea animals were eating up the beds of kelp. Scientists wondered why there were many more sea urchins than there had been before.

They soon found the answer. Sea otters feed on millions of sea urchins each year, but people were killing sea otters to get their fur. Without sea otters, the sea urchin population grew. People had upset the balance among kelp, sea urchins, and otters. Laws now protect the sea otter from being hunted. This helps to keep the kelp beds safe from the sea urchins.

Objective

A to explain how people upset the ecology of an environment

Check Up

A People killed _____ for their fur. Then there were too few left to keep down the number of _____. As a result, these sea animals grew in number and ate up the _____ beds.

B Oceanographers and How They Study the Ocean

You know that oceanography is the study of the oceans. **Oceanographers** are scientists who study oceans.

For example, oceanographers study the surface waters of the ocean. They take the temperature of the water with a thermometer. In this way they can find warm and cold currents in the ocean and tell which way the currents move. They also check for poisons in the water. If they find poisons, they warn people not to eat the fish caught in those waters.

Scientists have been studying the surface waters of the ocean for many years. Now they are able to study the bottom of the ocean as well. They have discovered many things about the ocean bottom. Do you know that there are hot springs on the bottom of the ocean? Oceanographers know a lot about these springs. The springs allow some plants to grow deep in the ocean. Giant clams and worms feed on these plants. Fish and crabs feed on the worms and clams. A whole food chain depends on these hot springs.

Oceanographers are able to study the ocean floor because of all the new equipment, or tools, they now have.

Check Up

B1 Oceanographers measure water temperature to find out how _____ in the ocean move.

Objectives

B1 to describe what oceanographers have learned about ocean surface waters

B2 to describe what oceanographers have learned about the ocean bottom

Oceanographers gather information from the bottom of the sea.

B2 Oceanographers have discovered _____ on the ocean bottom. These _____ allow some plants to grow on the ocean _____.

Scuba diving equipment is a tool of the oceanographer. Scuba divers explore underwater environments. Their equipment includes many things. They wear rubberlike suits called wet suits to keep warm. They carry one or two tanks of air on their backs. Tubes lead from the tanks to the divers' mouths. When underwater, scuba divers must remember to breathe in and out through their mouths, not through their noses.

The divers wear fins to help them swim better. A face mask protects their eyes. They wear belts with weights to keep them underwater. Scuba divers cannot go into very deep ocean. The pressure of the water would crush them.

Oceanographers also use submarines to study the deep ocean. A **submarine** is an underwater boat. It can go into much deeper water than a scuba diver can. A submarine has very thick glass windows. Bright lights are fastened to the outside. Underwater the lights are turned on. The oceanographers can look through the glass windows. They can take pictures of life in the deep ocean. Their tools are helping oceanographers learn more about the ocean.

Check Up

B3 Scuba divers wear a _____ to keep warm. A _____ is worn to protect their eyes. They wear _____ to help them swim. Belts with _____ keep scuba divers underwater.

B4 Divers cannot go very deep because the _____ of the water would crush them.

B5 Oceanographers use submarines because they can go into _____ than scuba divers can.

Objectives

B3 to list what equipment scuba divers wear

B4 to recognize why scuba divers cannot go into deep ocean

B5 to tell how submarines help oceanographers

Scuba divers wear special protective gear. The oxygen tanks on this diver's back help him stay under water for a long time.

219

Each year millions of fish are taken from the oceans.

C Riches from the Ocean

The ocean is the main source of food for millions of people. Some countries do not have the land to raise cattle for meat. People in these countries depend on fish from the ocean for food. Each year people take millions of animals and plants from the ocean. Besides the plants and animals that are food for many people, there are other useful things in the ocean.

How much salt do you think there is in the ocean? If all the salt were taken out of the ocean, it would cover every bit of land on earth to a depth of more than 150 meters. People cannot drink ocean water as it is. Ways have been found to take the salt out of sea water, but the cost is high.

Ocean salt has **chlorine,** which is used in drinking water and in swimming pools. **Magnesium,** an important metal, is also found in ocean salts. Many minerals that are used to make metals are found on and below the ocean floor. Scientists are trying to find a way to take them out.

Oceanographers have found that there are many useful things in ocean waters and on the ocean floor. Now many countries of the world are arguing about the use of the oceans. To whom do the oceans belong? There are different answers to that question. No one answer has been accepted by every country. It is a problem still to be solved.

Check Up

Objectives

C1 to describe how people use the plants and animals of the ocean

C2 to explain why countries are arguing about the use of the ocean

C1 People use ocean animals and plants for _____.

C2 Because there are so many _____ things in the oceans, countries argue about who owns them.

D Oil in the Ocean Floor

Can you think of reasons we need energy? We need energy to heat our homes and cook our food. We need energy to run our cars, buses, planes, and trains. Most of the energy we use comes from oil. We are running out of oil in the United States.

Oil has been discovered beneath the ocean floor. To get this oil, special platforms are built in the water. Big drills are set up on the platforms. The drills dig deep holes into the ocean floor to bring up the oil. Sometimes accidents happen and oil spills into the water.

Oil is lighter than water. It floats on top of the ocean. Water birds get this oil on their feathers. This keeps the birds from flying. As a result many birds die.

Oil washed on shore in the wetlands can coat plants. Covered with oil, these plants cannot get the sunlight they need and they die. The oil also can kill the tiny animals of the wetlands. This is a very serious problem. Remember that the living things in wetlands are important to all ocean life.

Objectives

D1 to explain why companies are drilling for oil in the ocean

D2 to explain why oil spills are dangerous

Check Up

D1 Companies are drilling for oil in the ocean

because we are _____ of oil in the United States.

D2 Oil spills can kill plants, _____, and the

tiny animals that live in the _____.

This is an offshore drilling platform. Water pollution from oil spills is increasing.

E Pollution of the Water and the Beach

Objectives

E1 to recognize why tuna and swordfish can be unsafe to eat

E2 to explain how towns and cities pollute the water

E3 to describe how careless people pollute beaches

You may have seen a sign like this one in your area. It warns the children not to swim in the polluted water.

Not too long ago, some swordfish and tuna were found to contain a lot of mercury. **Mercury** is dangerous to humans. So these fish were not safe to eat. Where did this mercury come from?

For many years factories have been polluting our waters by dumping wastes into rivers. Some of the waste materials contain mercury. The rivers carrying the polluted waste flow into the ocean. Plankton eat the waste. Small fish eat the plankton. Tuna and swordfish eat the small fish. Mercury collects in the bodies of tuna and swordfish. When this happens, the fish are unsafe to eat.

The government has passed laws to stop this mercury pollution. Slowly the amount of mercury in the ocean is getting less. Most swordfish and tuna are safe to eat now.

Cities and towns also add to water pollution. They empty **sewage,** or human wastes, into the ocean. In some places near the shore, clams and oysters are poisoned from the sewage. They become unsafe to eat. Sometimes beaches are closed to swimming because there is too much sewage in the water.

Litter is a kind of pollution. Many careless people leave garbage and trash on beaches and other public places. These people are litterbugs. Do you litter? What can you do to stop others from littering?

Check Up

E1 Some swordfish and tuna are unsafe to eat because they contain _____. This material is poisonous to humans and comes from factory waste.

E2 Towns and cities pollute by dumping _____ into the ocean.

E3 Careless people _____ the beaches with garbage and trash.

Discover for Yourself

How do we know that there are salts dissolved in water?

Materials

- pan
- salt
- water
- hot plate

Procedure

1. Put about 200 mL of water in a clean pan, and your teacher will put it on the hot plate. Heat until all the water evaporates. Record the results of this part of the experiment below.
2. Now put about 200 mL of water in the pan, but dissolve as much salt in the water as you can. Make sure there are no salt crystals left in the bottom of the pan and then put it on the hot plate. Evaporate the water. Record the results of this experiment below.

Results

1. What was left in the pan after you evaporated the tap water? _____

2. Where did it come from? _____

3. Why didn't it evaporate with the water? _____

_____

4. What was left in the pan after you evaporated the salty water? _____

5. Did the salt in the pan look like the salt that you started with? _____

6. Why do you think the salt looked as it did after the water had evaporated? _____

_____

Chapter Summary

- Ecology is the study of relationships in the environment.
- People can upset the balance of nature by removing large numbers of some plant or animal from its environment.
- Oceanographers study the surface waters of the ocean to learn about currents and poisons in the water.
- New equipment has helped oceanographers study the ocean floor.
- The ocean is the main source of food for millions of people.
- Salt and valuable minerals are found in ocean waters and on the ocean floor.
- Oil is being taken from the ocean floor. Oil spills are a serious problem for life in the oceans and wetlands.
- Polluted ocean waters can make many ocean animals unsafe to eat.
- Sewage and litter add to pollution in and around water.

An Ocean Teacher

Jacques-Yves Cousteau is an oceanographer from France. He studies the ocean waters. He learns about the plants and animals that live in the ocean. He also explores the ocean floor. Cousteau learns about the ocean so he can teach others. His hope is to make people understand how important the oceans are.

When Cousteau started studying the oceans, there were very few tools for oceanographers to use. He soon knew that people needed better equipment. Cousteau helped invent the aqualung. This is an air tank a person uses to breathe underwater. He had the idea for a small submarine to carry one person near the ocean floor. Cousteau also had a special kind of room built for people to live in underwater. From this room they could study the ocean for several weeks at a time.

Jacques Cousteau has a large ship called the *Calypso.* He and his crew sail it around the world to

Jacques Cousteau is shown here in one of his ocean-going vessels.

study the oceans. They make movies and television shows and write books about what they find. Cousteau thinks that healthy oceans are important to our future. He wants everyone to learn more about the ocean biome so people will treat the oceans with care.

Problem Solving

If you have ever been swimming in the ocean you know how salty it is. Most inland lakes and rivers are not salty. They are called "fresh water."

Why are lakes "fresh" while oceans are salty? Where did the salt come from? Do you think that the oceans are getting saltier or less salty?

Step 1 Make a problem solving plan. Discuss the questions with the class.

Step 2 Gather information. Read about the oceans' salt water.

Step 3 Organize your information. Find out what sources of salt there are in and around the oceans.

Step 4 Analyze your information. Where does the salt come from?

Step 5 Generalize. How could the oceans become more salty? How could they become less salty?

Step 6 Make a decision. Based on what you have learned about the source of salt in the ocean, do you think that the oceans will become more salty as time goes on, or less salty?

Test Yourself

In each sentence there is a word, or words, missing. Look for the missing word(s) in the list at the side of the page. Then, fill in the blank with the correct word(s).

1. Oceanographers often use _____ to explore the very deep ocean.

2. Spiny animals called _____ feed on kelp.

3. Divers wear wet suits to keep their bodies

_____.

4. Divers wear _____ on their feet to help them swim.

5. Dumping sewage into the oceans causes water

_____.

6. People who wear wet suits and carry air tanks to go into the oceans are called _____.

7. Salt from the sea contains a material called

_____ that is used in swimming pools.

8. Some fish have been found to contain a lot of

_____ from factory wastes.

sea urchins
scuba divers
fins
submarines
chlorine
mercury
pollution
warm

Circle the letter in front of the word that best completes the sentence.

1. Sea urchins feed on _____.

    (a) otters
    (b) whales
    (c) kelp

2. Scuba divers wear _____ to protect their eyes.

    (a) tanks
    (b) fins
    (c) masks

3. Because it is lighter than water, _____ floats on the surface.

    (a) oil
    (b) salt
    (c) chlorine

Pronunciation Guide

When you read science material, you often come across words that are unfamiliar to you or difficult to pronounce. In this book, new or difficult science words appear in a special kind of type called **boldface** type. The Glossary in the back of this book contains a list of these boldface words. Those words which are difficult to pronounce are spelled according to the way they are said. The key below will help you say these words correctly.

Pronunciation Guide

Letters	Show the Sound of	Written as	Letters	Show the Sound of	Written as
a	cat	KAT	oh	go	GOH
ah	odd	AHD	oo	moon	MOON
ahr	bar	BAHR	or	store	STOR
aw	lawn	LAWN	ow	out	OWT
ay	pay	PAY	oy	joy	JOY
b	bib	BIB	p	pop	PAHP
ch	chip	CHIP	r	rat	RAT
d	deed	DEED	s	see	SEE
e	pet	PET	sh	ship	SHIP
ee	bee	BEE	t	tin	TIN
er	care	KER	th	thing	THING
eye	island	EYE luhnd	th	then	THEN
f	fast	FAST	u	book	BUK
g	gag	GAG	uh	cut	KUHT
h	hat	HAT	ur	her	HUR
i	pit	PIT	v	vase	VAYS
ir	dear	DIR	w	with	WITH
j	joke	JOHK	y	yet	YET
k	kit	KIT	z	zebra	ZEE bruh
l	lid	LID	zh	vision	VIZH uhn
m	man	MAN			
n	no	NOH			
ng	thing	THING			

Primary Stress is shown by capital letters—**axis** shown as AK sis.

Glossary

A

abyssal (uh BIS uhl) **plain:** flat part of the ocean floor

adaptation (ad uhp TAY shuhn): part or behavior of a plant or animal that helps it to stay alive in its environment

air pollution (puh LOO shuhn): addition of harmful things to air

alcohol (AL kuh hawl): liquid substance harmful to the body

alga (AL guh): simple plant with no true roots, stems, or leaves

alnico: mixture of aluminum, nickel, and cobalt used to make a strong magnet

animal plankton (PLANGK tuhn): tiny water animals that float near the surface

Antarctica (ant AHRK ti kuh): region around the South Pole

antiseptic (an ti SEP tik): medicine to kill germs on the skin

Arctic (AHRK tik): region around the North Pole

atmosphere (AT muhs fir): air that surrounds the earth

atoll (A tawl): coral island

atom (AT uhm): tiny piece of matter

auditory (AW duh tor ee) **nerve:** nerve that carries vibrations from the inner ear to the brain

axis (AK sis): imaginary line that runs from the North to the South Pole through the center of the Earth

B

biome (BEYE ohm): area with one kind of climate

bladder (BLAD ur): baglike part of seaweed that floats

boil: change to gas by adding heat

breads and cereals (SIR ee uhlz) **group:** one of the four healthy food groups

burrow (BUR oh): underground home of an animal

C

cable (KAY buhl): thick wire

caffeine (ka FEEN): chemical found in coffee, tea, and cola that can harm your body

canopy layer (KAN uh pee LAY ur): the highest part of a forest made up of tall treetops

caption (KAP shuhn): words under, above, or beside a picture

carnivorous (kahr NIV ur uhs): meat eating

chlorine (KLOR een): substance found in ocean salt

circuit (SUR kit): path that carries electricity

climate (CLEYE muht): kind of weather a place has over a long period of time

closed circuit: path that is complete and that electricity can flow through

cloud: mass of water vapor and dust particles in the air

coastal plain: flat land near the edge of a continent

compass (KUHM puhs): instrument that helps tell direction

conductor: material that electricity can flow through easily

cone (KOHN): plant part that holds seeds of a coniferous tree

coniferous (kuh NIF ur uhs): tree that stays green all year long and has cones

consumer (kuhn SOOM ur): animal or plant that depends on other animals or plants for food

continent (KAHN tuh nuhnt): one of several large land areas on the earth

continental rise (kahn tuh NEN tuhl REYEZ): ocean floor gradually sloping up to base of continental slope

continental shelf: gently sloping underwater plain at the edge of most continents

continental slope (SLOHP): steep drop of the ocean floor at the edge of the continental shelf

cool-down exercise: exercise that helps relax muscles

coral (KOR uhl): tiny sea animals

cornea (KOR nee uh): clear covering over the front of the eye

current (KUR uhnt): movement of water in rivers and oceans

D

decay (di KAY): rot

deciduous (di SIJ oo wuhs): plant that loses its leaves in the fall

den: cave or other place where animals sleep

desert: a place where there is very little rainfall

dune (DOON): rounded hill of sand shaped by the wind

E

ear: sense organ for hearing

ear canal (kuh NAL): tunnel in the ear leading to the eardrum

eardrum: part of the ear that sound waves strike

ecological reserve (EE kuh LAWJ i kuhl ri ZURV): large area of land set aside for wildlife

ecology (ee KAHL uh jee): study of living things in their environment

electrical shock (i LEK tri kuhl SHAHK): painful jolt of electricity

environment (in VEYE ruhn muhnt): living and nonliving things around you

evaporate (i VAP uh rayt): change from liquid to vapor

eye: sense organ for sight

eyeglasses (EYE glas uhz): device to help some people see better

eyelashes (EYE lash uhz): hairs that help keep foreign objects out of the eyes

exercise: something you do to move, stretch, and use your body

expand (ik SPAND): get bigger

extinct (ik STINGKT): no longer living

F

fats, sweets, and alcohol (AL kuh hawl) **group:** the fifth and unhealthy food group

fault: crack in the earth's crust

fault-block mountains: mountain formed when the crust of the earth moves along a fault

fertile (FUR tuhl): rich

fin: part of a fish that helps it to move through water

folded mountain: mountains formed when the crust of the earth folds because of pressure

food chain: group of plants and animals that depend on each other for survival

food group: group of foods that give some of the needed nutrients

force: a push or a pull

forest floor: ground made up of soil and dead leaves

freeze: change to ice

frond (FRAHND): leaflike part of seaweed that allows water to enter

fruits and vegetables group: one of the four healthy food groups

fungus (FUHNG guhs): nongreen plant that cannot make its own food

G

gas: the state in which matter can change both its shape and volume

generator (JEN uh rayt ur): machine that makes electricity

gill: part of a fish that takes in oxygen from the water

goggles (GAHG uhlz): special glasses to protect eyes

grassland: area that gets between 50 and 65 centimeters of rainfall a year

H

hearing: sense that allows us to pick up sounds

herb (URB) **layers:** flowers, grasses, mosses, and mushrooms that grow near the forest floor

herbivorous (hur BIV ur uhs): plant eating

high tide (TEYED): highest level of water in the ocean

holdfast: plant part that holds seaweed on the ocean floor

I

image (IM ij): upside-down picture of what you see

inner (IN ur) **ear:** part of the ear that sends vibrations to the auditory nerve

iris (EYE ris): colored part of the eye surrounding the pupil

irrigation (ir uh GAY shuhn): process of bringing water to dry land

K

kelp: a kind of brown seaweed

L

lava (LAH vuh): magma that erupts through the surface of the earth

lens (LENZ): part of the eye that focuses light

lichen (LEYE kuhn): simple plant made up of an alga and a fungus

liquid (LIK wid): a fluid, such as water

litter (LIT ur): garbage and trash left in public places

lodestone (LOHD stohn): magnetic rock

lodge (LAHJ): beaver home made out of branches, twigs, and mud

low tide: lowest level of water in the ocean

M

magma (MAG muh): melted rock deep within the earth

magnesium (mag NEE zee uhm): important metal found in ocean salts

magnetic (mag NET ik): attracts certain metals

magnetite (MAG nuh teyet): kind of iron in magnetic rocks

matter: anything that takes up space and has mass

meat group: one of the four healthy food groups

mercury (MUR kyur ee): metal that can be dangerous to living things

mid-Atlantic ridge (mid ut LANT ik RIJ): mountains on the floor of the Atlantic Ocean

middle ear: part of the ear with three small bones that send vibrations to the inner ear

migrate (MEYE grayt): move

milk and dairy (DER ee) **group:** one of the four healthy food groups

mineral (MIN ur uhl): nutrient found in food

mollusk (MAHL uhsk): type of water animal usually having a shell or pair of shells

moss (MAHS): simple plant that grows on tree trunks and rocks

N

needle: leaf of a coniferous tree

nerve (NURV): pathway connecting a sense organ to the brain

nerve ending: part of nerve that reacts to stimuli

new mountains: mountains with sharp, rocky peaks

noise (NOYZ): unpleasant or unwanted sound

nonconductor (nahn kuhn DUHK tur): material that electricity cannot flow through easily

nose: sense organ for smell

nostril (NAHS truhl): opening in the nose where air enters

nut: seed of some trees

nutrient (NOO tree uhnt): part of food needed for growth and energy

O

oasis (oh AY sis): a place in the desert where there is water

ocean: large body of salt water

oceanographer (oh shuh NAHG ruh fur): scientist who studies the ocean

oceanography (oh shuh NAHG ruh fee): study of oceans and seas

old mountains: rounded mountains that have been worn down by wind and water

open circuit (SUR kit): path that is broken and that electricity cannot flow through

optic (AHP tik) **nerve:** nerve that carries messages from the retina to the brain

orbit (OR buht): circular path around a heavenly body

outer (OWT ur) **ear:** part of the ear that picks up sound waves from the air

oxygen (AHK si juhn): gas that living things need to breathe

P

permanent magnet (PUR muh nuhnt MAG nit): magnet that keeps its magnetism for a long time

plankton (PLANGK tuhn): tiny water plants and animals

plant plankton: tiny water plants that float near the surface

polar region (POH lur REE juhn): very cold area around the North or South Pole

pole: end of a magnet

pollution (puh LOO shuhn): harmful things in the environment

pond: body of water usually smaller than a lake

power station: place where electricity is stored

prairie (PRER ee): grassland

producer (pruh DOO sur): plant that makes its own food

property (PRAHP ur tee): characteristic of a substance that tells what it is like and how it acts

protective coloration (pruh TEK tiv kuhl uh RAY shuhn): adaptation that helps a plant or animal blend into its surroundings

pupil (PYOO puhl): round opening in the center of the eye

R

rain forest: forest in hot, moist climate

reptile (REP teyel): animal with scales whose blood temperature is affected by the environment

retina (RET uhn uh): lining of the back part of the eyeball

revolve (ri VAHLV): make a complete path around another object

rotate (ROH tayt): spin

S

satellite (SAT uh leyet): an object in space that travels around another object

scale (SKAYL): flat piece that makes up the covering of a fish or a reptile

school: group in which fish travel

sea: large body of salt water

seaweed: algae growing in the ocean

seed: part of plant from which a new plant can grow

sense: sight, hearing, touch, taste, or smell

sense organ: part of the body that picks up changes in the environment

shrub (SHRUHB) **layer:** woody-stemmed plants that grow close to the ground

simple plant: plant with no true roots, stems, or leaves

skim: look quickly through reading material to find out something you want to know

skin: organ that covers the body

slime (SLEYEM): sticky material found on skin of most fish

smell: odors in the air to which nerves in the nose react

soil pollution (SOYL puh LOO shuhn): addition of harmful things to the soil

solar system (SOH lur SIS tuhm): system of planets and other space objects revolving around the sun

solid (SAHL uhd): form of matter that has a definite size and shape

sound: result of vibration of an object

sprout (SPROWT): grow

stimulus (STIM yuh luhs): anything that causes nerve endings to react

submarine (SUHB muh reen): underwater boat

suction disk (SUHK shuhn DISK): flat, round disc on octopus tentacle; used for catching and holding food

survive (sur VEYEV): stay alive

T

taste: reaction of nerve endings on the tongue

taste bud: nerve ending for taste on the tongue

tears (TIRZ): salty liquid in the eyes

temporary magnet (TEM puh rer ee MAG nit): magnet that keeps its magnetism for a short time

tentacle (TEN tuh kuhl): long arm of an octupus

thaw: melt

tide (TEYED): rise and fall of ocean water

tobacco (tuh BAK oh): harmful material in cigarettes

tongue (TUHNG): sense organ for taste

touch: reaction of nerve endings in the skin

trench: long, narrow cut in the ocean floor

tundra (TUHN druh): plain between northern coniferous forest and the Arctic Circle

turbine (TUR buhn): large wheel with blades that is used to turn a generator

U

understory layer: the part of the forest made up of the tops of smaller trees

V

vibration (veye BRAY shuhn): back and forth movement that produces sound

vine (VEYEN): plant that curls, twines, and twists

vitamin (VEYET uh min): a nutrient found in food

volcano (Vahl KAY noh): cone-shaped mountain formed from lava erupting through the earth's surface

W

warm-up exercise: exercise that stretches your muscles

water pollution (puh LOO shuhn): addition of harmful things to water

water vapor (VAY pur): water in the air in the form of a gas

wave: kind of water movement caused by the wind

wetland: muddy shore

wind: movement of air

Index